OVERCOMING

Portraits of Faith and Victory

BILL CROWDER

ALICE MATHEWS

DAVID ROPER

D1040527

DISCOVERY HOUSE

P U B L I S H E R S ®

Overcoming
© 2011 RBC Ministries

Discovery House Publishers is affiliated with
RBC Ministries, Grand Rapids, Michigan 49512

Cover Design: Stan Myers
Cover Photo by iStock

Printed in the United States of America
First Printing 2011

CONTENTS

PREFACE

he ancient patriarch Job, no stranger to hardship and pain, wisely observed, "Man is born to trouble as surely as sparks fly upward" (Job 5:7). To further affirm this idea, he also declared, "Man born of woman is of few days and full of trouble" (Job 14:1). It is not difficult to see that little has changed in the thousands of years since Job penned those words out of his own season of grief and loss. Yet, in the midst of reminding us of the inevitability of struggle in this life, he affirmed confidence in his God by saying, "Though He slay me, yet will I hope in Him" (Job 13:15).

For Job and for us, it is this confidence in God that can enable us to endure and even to know victory in the darkest seasons of life. This confidence is born out of the experiences of life that teach us of God's presence, remind us of God's power, and encourage us with God's faithfulness. These experiences teach us that, as the praise chorus says, "Life is hard, but God is good."

The goodness of God, learned through the badness of life in a fallen and broken world, was not the sole property of Job, however. It was the repeated experience of many other men and women in the Bible. From Joseph and Hannah in the Old Testament to Mary and Martha in the New Testament (and others besides), the joy of victory in times of challenge reminds us that God is truly sufficient for whatever life may throw at us.

We invite you to join us in learning the lessons of overcoming through the stories of seven Bible people and in embracing the God who alone can bring good out of the worst things in this world (Romans 8:28; Genesis 50:20). It is His goodness and care that can teach us, as it did with them, that overcoming is possible because "His love endures forever" (Psalms 136:1).

—Bill Crowder

Associate Bible Teacher
RBC Ministries

One

JOSEPH

Overcoming Life's Challenges

 he football coach was to the point of exasperation: "Losing five games in a row is bad enough. But what really frustrates me is that we keep making the same mistakes over and over. We just aren't learning anything!"

Wasting the pain of failure happens off the field as well. We can be slow to learn that what causes the most pain is not the initial loss or hardship but the failure to learn in the process. If we really believe that God is working all things for our good, then one of the great challenges is to allow hard, painful, and tear-filled experiences to be our teacher in the classroom of life.

Old Testament character Joseph learned through difficult circumstances how to overcome. It's my prayer that by examining his story we can learn some vital lessons about life's challenges.

—*Bill Crowder*

The Lessons of Life

ON THE OLD *HAPPY DAYS* television show, Richie Cunningham had just been "grounded for life" by his father, Howard, for misbehavior. As they talked about it, Howard asked his son, "Did you know that there is a lesson in this for you?" Richie's response was priceless: "I figured anything with this much pain had to have a lesson in it somewhere."

That is real life! We do not learn character in times of ease and prosperity but in times of difficulty. The greatest lessons of life are often the product of our most serious heartaches.

When my father died, a pastor friend came to the funeral home. I had been a pastor only a few months, and my father's funeral would be the first that I would preach. My friend put his arm around my shoulder and said, "I know this hurts an awful lot—and it should. But one day you will be thankful for the lessons you learn this week." He continued, "I have never lost anyone close to me, but I have preached scores of funerals. Never in those funerals have I felt the ability to truly comfort people in the time of their greatest loss because I have never experienced that pain. What you will learn in your pain will enable you to minister far more effectively to the pain of others."

In one of the most practical books in the New Testament, James wrote these words:

> *Consider it pure joy, my brothers, whenever you*
> *face trials of many kinds, because you know that*
> *the testing of your faith develops perseverance.*
> *Perseverance must finish its work so that you may be*
> *mature and complete, not lacking anything (1:2-4).*

His point is simple—God doesn't waste anything! Everything happens in our lives for a reason, and a great part of that reason is to help us grow in our faith.

It has been said that life has to be lived in a forward motion but can only be understood by looking back. This demands that we trust in the loving purposes of a sovereign God. We must trust that He is in control—especially when life seems to be out of control.

This is what Paul referred to as walking by faith (2 Corinthians 5:7). It goes against every element of self-preservation that is ingrained in us. We want to take charge, manipulate, and control. But God wants us to trust in the love of a Father who makes no mistakes. He wants us to rely on the One who makes us "more than conquerors through him who loved us" (Romans 8:37).

Such was the life of the Old Testament character Joseph. His life was filled with dark, difficult experiences—yet the final outcome was amazing! In fact, Joseph is able to teach us much about how to deal with the tangled threads of our own lives. He became a godly man in an ungodly culture—a true overcomer—and his example can help prepare us as we face the issues of life.

Overcoming Life's Challenges

■ OVERCOMING TREACHERY

THERE ARE MANY BEAUTIFUL WORDS in the English language—words that are almost musical in their sound. *Treachery* is not one of those words.

When we hear the word *treachery*, we think of Benedict Arnold, who sold out his fledgling nation almost before it was born. We hear Caesar, in anguish from the knife planted firmly in his back, as he cries, "Et tu, Brute?" When we hear the word *betrayal*, our minds flash back to a garden on a dark night, the voice of a friend, and a kiss that sold out the Son of God for thirty pieces of silver.

As we enter the life of Joseph, he is standing at the very threshold of treachery—a betrayal that will rise up out of his own family. It will carry with it short-term pain for him, but it is a lesson in overcoming that young Joseph must learn.

The Seedbed For Tension. I remember years ago making a call on a family who had visited our church. As soon as I entered the house, I sensed the tension in the air. It was uncertain whether anyone in the family had love for anyone else, but it was abundantly clear that they did not like one another. In the course of the next 45 minutes, two things became obvious—the husband and wife were far from being on speaking terms with each other, and their personal civil war had migrated from their relationship to their children.

We assume that families will be places of warmth, love, acceptance, and security. But far too often, they don't live up to their billing. They become breeding grounds for anger, resentment, and bitterness. Such was the case with Jacob's household as seen in Genesis 37.

Lighting The Fuse Of Family Anger. The patriarch Jacob, son of Isaac and grandson of Abraham, was learning the hard way that you really do reap what you sow. He had ignored the biblical pattern for marriage in Genesis 2 by taking multiple wives. He had children by these two wives (and their handmaids) and ended up with a mixed family of twelve sons, all vying for position with their father.

The problem was intensified by Jacob's obvious preference for his second wife, Rachel, and her two sons, Joseph and Benjamin. This created serious friction in the family. By being elevated to special status in the household, these two boys became outcasts in their own family.

In addition, Jacob's less-than-sterling character

was being reproduced in his sons. His name (Jacob) means "conniver," and Jacob's sons had learned at the feet of the master. The family was riddled with strife, deception, and self-interest. The explosive atmosphere was further destabilized by the poor parenting practices he displayed. Genesis 37 describes three points of potential combustion in the household:

- Jacob used Joseph to spy on the older brothers, who hated this "favorite son" (v. 2).
- Jacob made a display of his favoritism in the gift of a special tunic (v. 3).
- Jacob fed the anger of the sibling rivalry, but their anger was directed at Joseph, not at their father and his foolish actions (v. 4).

The growth of conflict between the brothers was rooted in the problems within the marriage. The same results are seen in 1 Samuel 1, where polygamy produced inevitable competition and conflict between the wives. Of course polygamy isn't necessary for conflict to occur. Any breakdown in the husband-wife relationship has serious spill-over effects on all the relationships in the home. When that relationship is coupled with misguided parenting that elevates one child above the rest as the object of love and praise, the results can be catastrophic.

By showing preference to Joseph, Jacob made two serious errors. First, he sent wrong signals to Joseph about his position in the family over his older brothers. Second, by inference he inflicted the pain of rejection on the sons who had once been the object of his attention but were now forgotten. The resulting tension created a relational powder keg whose fuse was about to be lit. Jacob's lack of wisdom and obedience had built a family filled with resentment and hate.

Speaking of family tension, I remember reading an excerpt from a will dated July 1, 1935. It said:

> *Unto my two daughters, Frances Marie and Denise Victoria, by reason of their unloving attitudes toward a doting father . . . I leave the sum of $1 each and a father's curse. May their respective lives be filled with misery, unhappiness, and sorrow. May their deaths be soon and of a lingering, torturous nature. May their souls rest in hell and suffer the torments of the damned for eternity.*

A family can be a breeding ground for hatred, and the effects can be destructive indeed. Jacob's indiscretions had doused his household with gasoline—and Joseph was about to strike a match!

The Brashness Of Youth. Joseph received a set of dreams that predicted his future rise to greatness. But instead of considering their importance and seeking to understand them, he flaunted them before his family—including the brothers who already hated him. Joseph made three critical errors in judgment:

• He was *indiscriminate*—he didn't recognize the troubled situation in his family.

• He was *insensitive*— he didn't consider the

impact of his actions on family members.

• He was *immature*— he didn't stop to think of the hurt that his actions could cause.

The result was that the tension and anger continued to mount. The missing character quality in Joseph's young life was discernment. While it was true that one day he would exercise dominion over his brothers, his actions proved that he wasn't ready for that job yet.

Joseph had to be prepared for the responsibility of leadership, and that preparation would come as he learned the role of a servant. Servant-leadership displays discernment, sensitivity, and maturity. This is true whether it be husbands and their wives, leaders in a church, supervisors with their employees, or civic leaders and citizens. There is a crying need in our generation for leaders with a servant's heart.

For the Christian in leadership, the question is always, "Are you using your position, or are you allowing God to use you in it?" To this end, someone penned "The Leader's Prayer":

> *Lord, when I'm wrong, make me willing to change. When I'm right, make me easy to live with. So strengthen me that the power of my example will far exceed the authority of my rank.*

Joseph had to develop the character of a leader, but it would come only through the lessons and experience of being a servant.

Looking Out For Numbers One Through Ten. In Genesis 37:12-27, Jacob sent Joseph to check on his brothers, and, not surprisingly, these ten brothers resented Joseph's very presence among them. The pressure escalated as they contemplated "Daddy's Favorite."

First we see that anger had replaced love, even to the point of murder (v. 18). And sarcasm had replaced appropriate speech (v. 19). Reuben attempted to intervene on Joseph's behalf but was rebuffed (vv. 21-22). Finally, the attack took place in several stages:

> *Joseph had to develop the character of a leader, but it would come only through the lessons of being a servant.*

• They took his coat (v. 23), the symbol of their resentment.

• They cast him into a pit (v. 24) to remove him from their sight.

• With hardened hearts, they sat down to enjoy a meal while their young brother languished alone in a dark pit (v. 25).

• They sold him into slavery (vv. 25-28), deciding that making a profit on Joseph's life was the proper end to this sad event.

Notice what the unresolved family tension had produced. The root of bitterness is hate (Matthew 5:21-22). The symptom of bitterness is sarcasm (James 3:1-8). The result of bitterness is manipulation—using people instead of loving them.

The Root Of Bitterness And Its Tragic Fruit. For those who have studied this biblical story, it is easy to say, "It's okay. Everything will turn out all right in the end." But look at the immediate pain that flowed from a family eaten up with hate. Reuben mourned for Joseph (and his own lack of courage). The brothers lied to their father and never escaped their personal guilt (see Genesis 42:22). Jacob, the deceiver, was now deceived, and he experienced a pain that refused to be comforted. He had reaped what he had sown. As he had deceived his father with a goat, he was now deceived by the same means.

The last result of this family bitterness was that Joseph was sold into slavery. It's interesting that he is the only one who is not described in the text as being troubled. He was in the best position of them all, because even though he was enslaved he was right where God wanted him. He was right where he had to be so that he could learn the lessons God wanted to teach him—lessons that would one day make him a great leader and enable him to overcome the treachery and betrayal of his own brothers.

Psalm 76:10 says, "Surely your wrath against men brings you praise." Ever faithful, God would take the evil of men in Joseph's life and use it for the good of Joseph and the glory of God.

■ OVERCOMING TEMPTATION

T O SAY THAT LIFE is filled with trials and temptations is, as sportscaster Howard Cosell used to say, to have "a marvelous grasp of the obvious." To realize, however, that these trials often come on the heels of our greatest successes may be to understand the very essence of what makes life so hard.

It's probably true that how we handle success says as much if not more about us than how we handle failure. In learning to overcome temptation, Joseph was going to be challenged with success and the temptations it brings. And he would demonstrate that the lessons of God were starting to take hold in his young but maturing heart.

In Genesis 39, we see the saga of Joseph's life take a fascinating turn. He had become the property of Potiphar (37:36), an officer of Pharaoh and the captain of the guard. It is here that Joseph, as a servant, would learn how to be a leader—with all of the ups and downs leadership brings.

The Power Of Testimony. Potiphar was "captain of the guard" (39:1). There is some discussion among Bible scholars as to what that role was. Some say he was a warden, others believe that he was captain of the palace guard, and still others say he was captain of the executioners. What we do know is that Potiphar was wealthy enough to have many servants and slaves (vv. 11,14), and he had now added Joseph to his collection. Joseph distinguished himself as a young man of skill and ability, but it became clear that those talents were not the key to his life. Genesis 39:2 gives us the real key: "The Lord was with Joseph." God's presence was the difference.

Imagine how painful it must have been at age seventeen, not only to have been torn from his family and sold into slavery but also to have his family do it! How easy it would have been to become embittered and hate-filled (like his brothers). But that didn't happen to Joseph. Although he was far from home, the presence of God was very real in his life. In fact, this is the theme of Genesis 39 (see vv. 2-3,21,23), and it had a dramatic impact on Potiphar. He could not help but recognize the presence of God in the life of this remarkable slave. Imagine how strong Joseph's testimony had to be for Potiphar, who was a pagan, not only to recognize and admire Joseph's character but also to attribute it to God rather than to Joseph.

The clear implication of the text is that Joseph was not bitter toward his brothers nor enslaved by his circumstances. He was content in the presence of God (cp. Hebrews 13:5-6 and Philippians 4:10-13). He didn't mourn his disappointment but became useful where he was. And God used that heart of faithfulness and contentment.

Potiphar recognized God's presence with Joseph (39:3), and he made this young slave the overseer of his entire household (vv. 4-6). Joseph now supervised all the other servants, handled public relations, oversaw finances, and was responsible for the provisions for the household (valuable training for a later assignment Joseph would receive).

Everything Joseph touched was blessed. Now, perhaps 10 years after being sold into slavery, Joseph was on top of the world. And now he was more vulnerable than ever to temptation.

The Power Of Temptation. Notice the closing words of Genesis 39:6, "Joseph was well-built and handsome." Now Potiphar's wife enters the scene. Her response? She "took notice of Joseph" (v. 7). She would have been right at home in modern America. A magazine survey polled 60,000 American women, and the results were stunning: Forty-seven percent said that they thought premarital sex was acceptable, and twenty-seven percent endorsed extramarital affairs. Potiphar's wife had the same mindset. She was attracted to this young man physically, so she offered herself to him.

Look at Joseph's response. He refused her advances because of a powerful set of convictions. These convictions were not learned from his father, Jacob, nor from his hate-filled brothers, nor in the courts of pagan Egypt. These convictions were learned in the presence of God. He not only battled temptation but he also had a battle plan that he would follow as Potipher's wife continued to pursue him.

He had the right concerns (vv. 8-9). He was concerned ethically that his actions not hurt others, in this case Potiphar. His master had entrusted him with much, and Joseph refused to violate that trust for a moment of pleasure. He also looked beyond the immediate to the ultimate, recognizing the consequences that such sin would have on his relationship with God (v. 9). He was concerned *spiritually*, because he understood that all sin is against God. The offer of sensual pleasure is not worth the price tag attached to it.

He had the right strategy (v. 10). He avoided contact with her. Joseph realized that he had to be aware of the lure of sin and avoid its opportunities. He had to be alert!

It's like the story of a man applying for a job as a telegraph operator. One by one the applicants went for their interview, and one by one they were rejected. Finally, it was his turn. As he responded to the interviewer's questions, he was distracted by a tapping sound the man made with his pencil. He alertly translated them into dots and dashes, told the man what he was sending, and was hired for the job.

He had the right escape route (v. 12). When Potiphar's wife finally got Joseph alone, he ran as far as he could as fast as he could, leaving his coat behind. What Samson, David, and Solomon did not do, Joseph did. He fled, keeping the courage of his convictions and his integrity intact. He exemplified Paul's advice to Timothy: "Flee the evil desires of youth" (2 Timothy 2:22). He didn't flirt with sin, argue with it, or reason with it. He fled from it.

In spite of the evil environment, the woman's persistence, and his limited personal spiritual training, Joseph resisted. How?

- He recognized that he belonged to God.
- He recognized sin's effect on others.
- He recognized sin as defiance against God.

This young man's godly character was continuing to be shaped. In a perfect world (or on a thirty-minute television sitcom), his commitment would have resulted in everyone living happily ever after. But real life doesn't operate that way. Life in a fallen world seldom rewards right living.

The Power Of Revenge. Have you heard of the fury of a woman scorned? Joseph lived it. He was ruled by principles, but she was ruled by passion.

And when she was rebuffed, her passions exploded in anger. She had her own strategy—revenge.

• Joseph was lied about to the men of the house (39:13-15)—the second time a coat had been used in a lie about Joseph.

• Joseph was lied about to Potiphar (vv. 16-18).

• Joseph was imprisoned again (vv. 19-20), and again it was undeserved.

Remember that Potiphar may have been the chief executioner. In ancient Egypt, the penalty for adultery was 1,000 lashes, but the penalty for rape was death. It's possible that Potiphar knew that his wife was lying. At the very least, he knew that such an accusation was out of character for this young man. But desperate to save face, he had to do something. So he imprisoned Joseph.

Joseph ended up in jail for doing the right thing. We protest, "It isn't fair!" And that's true. Often life isn't fair—but our responsibility is to do right and leave the consequences to God.

Now what of Joseph? He responded properly to his enslavement and to his temptation as well. How would he respond to this imprisonment?

The Presence Of God. Once again he found comfort in the presence of God: "The Lord was with him; he showed him kindness" (v. 21). It would have been easy to ask, "Why be good and do right if I end up here?" But Joseph didn't. He rested in God's presence, and God blessed him, even in prison (vv. 21-23).

Once again, Joseph began to learn what it means to overcome. He was learning from the pains, problems, dangers, and tests of life. All these things come into focus when we view them through the lens of God's sovereign purposes. Then we can trust His will and know His mercy.

Joseph's character was under construction as he was shaped by adversity, punished by men, and honored by God. Genesis 39 ends the way it began—with Joseph in bondage. Yet through it all, his solid faith in God's control had helped him overcome.

■ OVERCOMING DISAPPOINTMENT

DURING HIS professional baseball career, Joe Torre won a batting championship, a Gold Glove award for fielding skill, and was named the National League Most Valuable Player. Years later, when he was an announcer for the California Angels, he said during a broadcast that earlier in the evening a boy had stopped him with an interesting question. The young man asked Torre, "Did you used to be somebody?" How quickly we forget.

Sometimes we can be swallowed up by the expectation expressed by the question, "What have you done for me lately?" One NFL coach, after a ten-game winning streak, took it further. He said the expectation is no longer "What have you done for me lately?" It's become "What will you do for me next?" How quickly we forget.

Does Anyone Remember? It would certainly be understandable if Joseph had lapsed into self-pity at this point. He was imprisoned and treated harshly. Psalm 105:18 says of Joseph, "They bruised his feet with shackles, his neck was put in irons." All this for the crime of honoring his master and maintaining sexual purity.

But the Lord was still with him, and Joseph rose to a position of leadership— even in prison. God gave him favor with the jailer (Genesis 39:21), and the jailer entrusted everything under his authority to Joseph's care. Why? "Because the Lord was with Joseph and gave him success in whatever he did" (v. 23).

Joseph was still learning the lessons of leadership. And one of the lessons that is critical to the matter of overcoming is the lesson of patience. Although Joseph was unjustly imprisoned again, he went about the business of being useful where he was. He faithfully served and patiently waited because he was learning that he was not there by accident. He was not forgotten. God not only remembered Joseph but He also had a plan for him that included a tour of duty in the prison of Egypt.

The God Who Never Forgets. Joseph was in prison for a divine appointment. In Genesis 40:1, the pieces of the puzzle begin to come together.

Two of Pharaoh's officials—his royal butler and his royal baker—offended their ruler. These were not just household servants. In ancient times of palace intrigue and political assassinations, it was absolutely critical that these men be totally loyal. Somehow they had failed Pharaoh, so they were placed in the prison where Joseph was the head steward (vv. 2-3).

Notice who entrusted them to Joseph's care. It was the captain of the guard—Potiphar (v. 4; cp. 37:36). Joseph accepted the responsibility and began the task of serving these disgraced members of Pharaoh's court. This was not just some cosmic accident. It was a divine appointment. How necessary it is that we see this and embrace it. There is no such thing as a coincidence. God is in control of our lives. Nothing happens by accident. Everything occurs for a purpose.

When I was in college, I was faced with a dilemma. I was on the soccer team, but I was also involved in a traveling ministry. A scheduling conflict arose between the two activities. Both had events that I was committed to, and I had to choose between them. I chose the soccer game and began making arrangements for a substitute for the traveling ministry team. On the day before these conflicting events, I was injured in a soccer game and forbidden to play in the next game. Quickly, I reversed course and went with the traveling ministry team. On the day that I would have been playing soccer, I met the young woman who would later become my wife! After the fact, I learned that she had been a last-minute substitute on the trip. We met our life partners on a trip that, humanly speaking, neither of us was supposed to be on.

One of the great joys—and challenges—of life is to look expectantly for the hand of God in all of life's circumstances. Joseph and these two fallen royal officials converged in prison right on schedule for the perfect plan of God—though they certainly wouldn't have chosen those circumstances for themselves.

Lest We Forget. Don't miss this. In spite of (or perhaps because of) his own difficulty and hardship, Joseph had become sensitive to others, a quality that he previously lacked (Genesis 37). He looked at these men (40:6-7) and recognized their hurt and distress. How easy it would have been to turn away, thinking, "No one is caring about the mistreatment I have received. Why should I care about anyone else's?" But he didn't. Joseph's response to the disappointment of unjust imprisonment was twofold:

• Vertical—he didn't allow his circumstances to disrupt his relationship with God.

• Horizontal—he didn't allow his hurt to prevent him from caring about the hurts of others.

Joseph could have ignored them, but he didn't. He had the grace to set aside his personal adversity and help others who were hurting. Life is filled with disappointment and loss, but we can be overcomers by refusing to become self-absorbed and self-centered. Instead of wasting our energy in self-pity, we can invest our time in meeting the needs of others.

For example, a missionary couple in India saw their six children killed, so they raised 300 foster children. Following a tragic flood at Toccoa Falls, Georgia, a man whose wife and two children had died in the flood said, "Every time I wanted to cry, someone else needed help and I felt compelled to offer. I was so consumed with helping others that I had no time to worry about myself."

Is that how you respond to adversity and disappointment? Or do you become so consumed with your own pain that you are blind to the pain of others? Sensitivity to the needs of others can be deadened by preoccupation with personal disappointment. But that wasn't true of Joseph. He not only noticed and cared—but he also got involved.

Forget Me Not. Joseph interpreted the dreams of the two officials (vv. 8-19), making sure they knew that he was not the one who deserved the credit—but God. It's a notable contrast to chapter 37, when he lorded his dreams over his brothers. Now his trust was in the Lord, not in himself. After Joseph interpreted the butler's dream, he asked only that he would not forget him (40:14-15).

Three days later, both dreams were fulfilled— exactly as Joseph had interpreted them (vv. 20-22). Once again Joseph had set aside personal gain. And once again he had refused the path of selfishness. His care and concern for these men was marvelous in its expression of true humility and godly character.

And how was that sensitivity rewarded? "The chief butler did not remember Joseph, but forgot him" (40:23). Earlier, Joseph's purity was rewarded with imprisonment. Now his caring was paid back with insensitivity. And notice for how long—two full years (41:1).

Joseph was abandoned—this time by a friend, not an enemy, and for a long time, not a short one. It would have been easy for him to succumb to disillusionment and disappointment. But those are the results of putting our trust in men— and Joseph's trust was in the Lord. Even though the butler had forgotten Joseph, God hadn't. These are the times that build into us the indispensable character quality of patient trust. James 1:2-4 says that this can be learned only through trials. James teaches that without patience there will be no maturity; and without trials, delays, and disappointments there will be no patience. It has been said that a man is not a hero because he is braver than anyone else but because he is brave longer. Joseph had overcome treachery, temptation, and now, disappointment. The lessons of becoming an overcomer were taking shape in his life—and he was finally ready for God to use him in a special way.

■ OVERCOMING SUCCESS

YEARS AGO, Erwin Lutzer wrote a helpful little book titled *Failure: The Back Door To Success.* It could have been written about Joseph.

Many times, it takes years of failures and setbacks to become an "overnight success."

Abraham Lincoln is a classic example. He had two failed businesses, one nervous breakdown, endured the death of a sweetheart, and was defeated for public office no less than ten times over the space of almost thirty years. Then, incredibly, he was elected President of the United States. Years of failure had equipped him to deal with the heady air of the heights of power.

Those repeated reversals, apparent failures, and personal tragedies did not defeat Lincoln. They strengthened his character and commitment. So it was with Joseph. After thirteen years of reversals, failure, and tragedy, the light of day finally entered his cell. He had been forgotten by the royal butler for two full years. It was two years of continued suffering, pain, and solitude. But it was also two years of preparation and character development. Now the time for which Joseph had been prepared had arrived. Genesis 41 records what happened as the servant and the task converged in God's perfect timing.

Dreams You Would Like To Forget. The stage was set by a pair of dreams that Pharaoh experienced (41:1-8). These dreams spoke of a coming calamity for the nation, but their message was unclear and he was troubled by the uncertainty of them. Like the butler and baker two years before, Pharaoh sensed that these were beyond ordinary dreams. So he sought the wisest men of his kingdom to interpret them.

This exposes a significant principle in our spiritual living. Pharaoh was troubled by spiritual things that were beyond his grasp. But there was great danger in seeking spiritual answers in the wrong places. His wise men and magicians didn't know the God who was dealing with him, and their answers were inadequate for the turmoil in his heart.

There is a great spiritual hunger today. And into the vacuum of spiritual truth come cultists, false teachers, and false spiritual leaders who find that people's hunger makes them easy prey for eartickling deception.

Answers must be sought from God's revealed truth. The empty answers of false teachers are void of the necessary power to address true spiritual needs or answer the burning spiritual questions of the human heart. Until we are willing to accept the authority of God's truth in our lives, we will not have the answers we need for the things that trouble our hearts and minds.

A Dream Remembered. In the pressure of the failures of Pharaoh's wise men to interpret the dreams, the butler remembered someone who had succeeded (40:9-13). He recounted to Pharaoh the prison dreams and the accurate interpretation he had received from a Hebrew prisoner there. Now Joseph would come into contact with the third in a trilogy of "dream pairs"—all linked together.

- Dreams of dominion over his brothers.
- Dreams of the butler and the baker.
- Dreams of the grain and the cows.

It's amazing how these dreams fit together. The second pair of dreams put Joseph in contact with the third set of dreams, which then enabled the fulfillment of the first set of dreams.

The promises God made to Joseph thirteen years earlier had now come full circle. To the eyes of men, it may appear about thirteen years late in arriving. But in the sovereign plan of God it was right on time.

A Dream Come True. Pharaoh was out of options, so he called for Joseph. With Joseph's liberation (41:14-16) we see a second vital principle—godly character is unaffected by the harsh circumstances of life.

Undiminished by unfair treatment and years in prison, Joseph stepped forward with three evident qualities:

Dignity—"He shaved" (Egyptians were clean shaven) and he "changed his clothing" (v. 14). Joseph dressed in appropriate clothes to come before the king. He had a sense of propriety and decorum that years in prison could not erase.

Humility—"It is not in me" (v. 16). Joseph didn't use the situation for self-promotion. He didn't try to exalt himself as he had earlier in his life (Genesis 37:5-10). Through all that had happened, he learned to put his trust in the Lord, not in himself. As Scottish theologian James Denney (1856–1917) said, "No man can at the same time prove that he is clever and that Jesus Christ is mighty to save."

Faith—"God will give Pharaoh an answer" (v. 16).

Sounds like something Daniel (2:27-30) and Paul (Acts 26) would say in the future. Joseph expressed his faith and gave the glory to God. This must have seemed unusual coming from a prisoner and slave.

God's patient investment in the life of Joseph was now paying dividends. These first words spoken by Joseph after prison revealed that the lessons had been well learned.

A Dreamweaver At Work. Pharaoh told Joseph his dream (41:17-36). The failure of Pharaoh's wisest men set the stage for God's glory to be revealed through a common slave. What was beyond human reason was not beyond the all-knowing God.

The answer to the dreams? "God has revealed to Pharaoh what he is about to do" (v. 25). Joseph had learned that he could rest in the sovereignty of God. The double dream was confirmed and would be fulfilled because God is God. The ultimate lesson Joseph had learned through slavery, imprisonment, and mistreatment was that God is in control. He will do what He says, for He is in charge.

Joseph challenged Pharaoh to see the purposes of God and to plan accordingly—because if God said it, it would happen. Joseph boldly offered counsel to the ruler of the land, and it was wise counsel indeed. He told him to plan for the lean years by being frugal during the plentiful years. Joseph had proven the benefit of his training by seeing the need and responding to it wisely. As nineteenth-century British leader William Gladstone said, "A great statesman is a man who knows the direction God is going for the next fifty years!" Joseph did—when no one else had a clue.

The Dream Answered. Pharaoh made a decision that would change the ancient world. He appointed Joseph to oversee the food supplies of all of Egypt. Why? Because he saw in Joseph the single most important characteristic of a true leader. He was "a man in whom is the Spirit of God" (v. 38).

This gives us yet another principle to consider: The qualifications of a true leader are not merely physical—they are also spiritual. It is not just about talent or skill but about character and relationship with God as well. The key character qualities of a great leader (which took years of suffering to build into Joseph) are internal, not external. They deal with knowing God, not with being great.

Once again God's timing was perfect. Two years earlier, Joseph's ability to interpret dreams would have been a novelty. Now it was a national treasure. Joseph was raised to the position God had promised so many years before. He was exalted over all Pharaoh's house (vv. 40-45) and was ready to face and overcome the great tests that success brings to a leader. He was ready for:

• *Perseverance*—It would not be easy for a Hebrew to rule Egypt. The pressure would be intense, especially as the famine wore on.

• *Performance*—The skills Joseph had learned in small duties would now be applied to a major task.

- *Pride*—J. Oswald Sanders wrote, "Not every man can carry a full cup. Sudden elevation frequently leads to pride and a fall. The most exacting test of all is to survive prosperity."

But Joseph was ready for the pressure and the responsibility. He would overcome because God had prepared him. As Samuel Rutherford said, "Praise God for the hammer, the file, and the furnace. The hammer molds us, the file sharpens us, and the fire tempers us." Joseph experienced it all, and he was ready to be used of God.

■ OVERCOMING BITTERNESS

A T THE NUREMBERG WAR CRIMES TRIALS following World War II, one of the defendants, upon hearing the charges against him, responded to the prosecutor, "It is your word against mine." The prosecutor's answer was profound: "No, it's your word against the victim's. He survived and is prepared to testify against you."

It's certainly hard to visualize Joseph as a victim at this point, isn't it? He was now the second most powerful man on earth, and he had absolute control over the destinies of millions of people—including the brothers who had sold him into slavery so many years earlier.

Much had happened since Joseph rose to power (Genesis 41). The seven years of plenty predicted by Pharaoh's dreams had come and gone—and

Joseph's plan had worked to perfection.

The grain was stored, and now, in the midst of the seven years of famine, the world was coming to Pharaoh's (and to Joseph's) doorstep for food. In Genesis 42, Joseph's brothers came seeking food, and he provided it for them.

In the course of that meeting, he questioned them and discovered that their father and younger brother were still alive. Joseph then began to set the wheels in motion for a reunion. He sensed that his brothers had changed—but for the sake of Benjamin, he had to make sure. In the ensuing events, he forced them to return with Benjamin. Then he prepared for the final test. At the banquet referred to in chapter 43, he gave Benjamin five times more than the other brothers, and they didn't resent the kind of favoritism that they had despised so viciously in Joseph. Then he seemed to put Benjamin in harm's way to test them. Would they protect Benjamin or abandon him as they had abandoned Joseph twenty years earlier?

Only God can look at the heart (1 Samuel 16:7), so Joseph put in motion the test that would expose them and reveal how genuine their apparent change really was.

A Plan For The Test (44:1-13). After the feast, Joseph commanded his butler to do several things: Fill their sacks with food, return their money, and put his silver cup in Benjamin's bag.

Why? The only way Joseph could test their character was to "return to the scene of the crime." They had to be put in the position of choosing between rescuing Benjamin at great personal risk and abandoning him to slavery for personal gain.

As soon as the brothers departed for Canaan, Joseph sent his servants to catch them and accuse them of the theft of the cup. The brothers reacted with shock and confusion. They claimed honesty based on the return of money they had found in their bags on the first trip for food. And they backed up their claims of honesty with a bold offer: "Kill the guilty one, and enslave the rest!"

The extreme nature of their offer was intended to prove their innocence and sincerity. They would certainly not make such an offer if even one of them was guilty. The steward's reply in verse 10 raised the stakes—and the pressure: "Whoever is found to have it will be my slave." Imagine the mounting tension as one by one the sacks were examined, and one by one found to contain only grain. The steward moved from elder to younger, and the stress of the moment reached its peak as they finally arrived at Benjamin's donkey.

Imagine the shock and pain as the cup was found in his sack. How could it be? They were so certain of their innocence. How would they respond? "They tore their clothes" (v. 13). They had reaped what they had sown, and in this dramatic gesture of mourning they displayed the depth of their grief and despair. They responded to Benjamin's distress the same way Jacob had responded years before when shown the bloody coat of colors that had belonged to Joseph.

Now the $64,000 question had to be answered. The agreement was that only the guilty would be enslaved and the rest could go home. The easy thing to do would be to leave Benjamin and go home. But they didn't. Envy and resentment no longer governed their thoughts and deeds. They returned with Benjamin, determined that whatever was to be faced they would face together. The evidence was there. They were truly changed men.

A Plea For Mercy (44:14-34). Notice the difference in their attitudes from years before:

• "They threw themselves to the ground before him" (v. 14), fulfilling the promise of Joseph's first set of dreams.

• "How shall we clear ourselves? God has found out the iniquity of your servants" (v. 16 NKJV). There were no excuses or rationalizations. There was no attempt to cover up. They admitted, through Judah, their guilt and submitted to slavery as a group. It was "we," not "he." Joseph tested them further with an offer of release, and they passed with flying colors.

• "Let [me] remain instead of the lad" (vv. 33-34 NKJV). What a turnabout! The same Judah who had led in the plan to sell Joseph offered to be Benjamin's substitute as a slave in Egypt. Why? Out of concern for their father (vv. 19-32). He openly acknowledged that the young man was now Jacob's favorite. But instead of resenting this favorite-son status, he longed to preserve it by giving himself.

Jesus said, "By their fruit you will recognize them" (Matthew 7:20), and the change in Judah was real. We have been examining God's work in the life of Joseph, but God had also been working in Judah and his brothers.

A Passionate Reunion (45:1-15). For Joseph, the years of pain dissolved in a moment of joy, and he wept uncontrollably in the presence of his brothers. They were tears of joy because his brothers had truly changed and tears of love because at last they were as brothers should be.

The room was electric as Joseph finally said the words that he had longed to say since he first saw them coming for food: "I am Joseph" (v. 3). But they were terrified. The dream had come true. Joseph had the power of life and death over them. What would he do? Notice his tenderness toward them:

• "He wept aloud" (v. 2), openly expressing his emotion.

• "Come close to me" (v. 4). They had been apart far too long.

• "Do not be distressed and do not be angry with yourselves" (v. 5). This was a time for joy.

• "God sent me" (vv. 5, 7-8). They were to trust that God was in control.

• "Go . . . and bring my father" (vv. 9,13 NKJV). It was time to share the joy. Forgiveness resolved the issue of guilt. Merrill Unger wrote, "Joseph displayed his deep faith in the omnipotence of God—overriding Satan, demonic powers, and wicked men to work out His sovereign will and unfrustratable plan.

"Faith lifted the whole sordid crime out of the pit of misery and self-recrimination and placed it on the mountain peak of divine sovereignty where God's forgiving grace not only heals but wipes away the past and the pain" (*Unger's Commentary On The Old Testament*, Moody Press, 1981, p. 94).

Joseph had overcome all these things—particularly the potential bitterness that would have seemed so normal. He exemplified grace, giving full forgiveness and no revenge. He exemplified love, discarding the wrongs of the past for the compassion of the present. He exemplified faith, trusting that God would preserve him from the bitterness that leads to self-destruction.

I was deeply moved when I read about Mr. and Mrs. Robert Bristol of Dearborn, Michigan. They traveled on their vacation to San Diego for the purpose of sharing Christ with a man in prison. The thing that made it so amazing was that this criminal was in jail for raping and murdering their precious daughter. That is a spirit of mercy born out of grace. It is full love that was not born out of ease or comfort or convenience, but out of suffering and hardship.

That's the only way to overcome bitterness. When we trust God and rest in Him, we can love others. Why? Because we believe in a God who is big enough to work in all things for our good.

The Trust That Overcomes

I N GENESIS 50:20, we read Joseph's final words to his brothers. They are a capsule of his life's view: "As for you, you meant evil against me; but God meant it for good, in order to bring it about as it is this day, to save many people alive" (NKJV). This amazing perspective reflected a life that had embraced the living God and trusted Him completely.

As you face the pains and heartaches and mistreatments of life, it is only by complete confidence in the goodness and plan of God that you can overcome. The things that could destroy you can become building blocks on the journey of faith as you look for the hand of God in all the circumstances of life. "This is the victory that has overcome the world, even our faith" (1 John 5:4).

If you have never confessed your sin and trusted Jesus Christ as your Lord and Savior, life can be a jumbled ball of confusion. But the One who died for your failures can bring rightness with God, forgiveness of sin, and a new sense of wholeness and purpose into your weary soul. Christ came into the world because of His love for you, and that love can bring an end to the emptiness or bitterness or sinfulness that wracks your life.

Accept by faith the gift of eternal life and personal forgiveness He offers, for the only way to really overcome forever is to accept the victory of Calvary that He accomplished for you. "The gift of God is eternal life in Christ Jesus our Lord" (Romans 6:23). Now *that* is real victory—and real overcoming.

Two

RUTH & HANNAH

Learning to Walk By Faith

The women of the Bible tell us a lot about ourselves. Although times have changed, human nature has not. Women as different as Ruth and Hannah can still help us see how to walk by faith.

In the following pages, author, Bible teacher, and professor Alice Mathews shows us that women like Ruth and Hannah are especially important because of what they tell us about our God. She also explores the timeless truth that in the wisdom and grace of God none of us lives above the power of a decision or beyond the reach of our Lord.

—*Martin R. De Haan II*

RUTH:
How To See God In The Dailiness Of Life

D O YOU ENJOY READING? It is my greatest joy and sometimes my besetting sin. I can lose myself in a good book when I should be doing other things. Most of us who enjoy reading know that a good story can take us out of the humdrum sameness of our lives and transport us into the tension and drama of someone else's experience.

I have a second question: Do you ever sneak a peak at the ending before you get there? If you're into a detective story and it's time to cook dinner, you may think you can't wait to find out who dunnit. So you look. Or if it's a great romance and you can't stand the thought that the wrong girl gets the boy, you may glance at the last page to see who ends up in his arms.

If you have ever sat down to read the little book of Ruth in the Old Testament, were you tempted to sneak a peak to see how the story ends? If you did, you were probably disappointed. The final verses of Ruth chapter 4—the climax of the whole story—seem anything but climactic. What we find there is a genealogy: "Perez was the father of Hezron, Hezron the father of Ram, Ram the father of Amminadab, Amminadab the father of Nahshon, Nahshon the father of Salmon," and so on. Can you imagine a duller ending for a story? An author would have to work hard to come up with something more boring and anti-climactic than that.

Yet, when we look at this little book of Ruth, we see a very good storyteller at work. All the way through we watch the author dropping hints of things to come—clues that draw us in, that keep us aware that the plot is thickening. Things could turn out several different ways. Why would the writer want to blow a good story with a bad ending?

To understand that those dull verses at the end of the book really are the climax—and a stunning climax at that—we have to go back and look at the rest of the story. Then, suddenly, a boring genealogy comes alive and makes sense.

Our story is a play in four acts. The five principal actors on our stage are three women—Naomi, Ruth, and Orpah—and two men—Boaz and the nearer kinsman. The stage director is God.

Act One. When the curtain goes up on the first act, we find a bitter old woman on center stage. To listen to her, it is clear that the Stage Director does not know what He is doing. But that's getting ahead of the story. Begin with the description of the setting as we read it in the script in Ruth 1:1-5.

In the days when the judges ruled, there was a famine in the land, and a man from Bethlehem in Judah, together with his wife and two sons, went to live for a while in the country of Moab. The man's name was Elimelech, his wife's name Naomi, and the names of his two sons were Mahlon and Kilion. They were Ephrathites from Bethlehem, Judah. And they went to Moab and lived there. Now Elimelech, Naomi's husband, died, and she was left with her two sons. They married Moabite women, one named Orpah and the other Ruth. After they had lived there about ten years, both Mahlon and Kilion also died, and Naomi was left without her two sons and her husband.

The setting is in the time of the judges. This period of Israel's history was one of barbaric oppression and bloodshed. Between violent invasions, tribal civil wars, and unchecked lawlessness, the Jews had to contend with constant trouble. Now a famine added to their misery. In Bethlehem—the House of Bread—there was no bread. Elimelech chose to take his family to neighboring Moab.

While the trip to Moab was not a long one—not much more than thirty miles east of Bethlehem—distance in the Bible, as H. W. Morton observed, is often measured not in miles but in distance from God. Moabites worshiped the god Chemosh, not Jehovah. Elimelech and his family left the familiar for the unfamiliar, the known for the unknown.

While in Moab, the family faced first the loss of the father, Elimelech. Then the sons who had both married Moabite women also died. The play begins with three widows in a gloomy, hopeless setting. Naomi, on center stage, has heard that once again Bethlehem is really the House of Bread. The famine has passed. Food is plentiful in Judah. She and her two daughters-in-law prepare to move to Bethlehem. The dialogue in our play begins in verse 8:

> Then Naomi said to her two daughters-in-law, "Go back, each of you, to your mother's home. May the Lord show kindness to you, as you have shown to your dead and to me. May the Lord grant that each of you will find rest in the home of another husband."

Naomi knew that Orpah and Ruth faced a bleak and uncertain future if they returned to Bethlehem with her. They must stay in Moab. She kissed them—a sign of release from any obligation to her. They had voluntarily stayed with Naomi after their husbands had died, but now they could not forfeit their own happiness just to care for her. Desperate, powerless to do anything for them, Naomi prayed that God would care for them and provide them with husbands who would care for them.

But note what Orpah and Ruth answered: "We will go back with you to your people." Whether out of loyalty to their dead husbands or out of love for their mother-in-law, Ruth and Orpah pushed on toward Bethlehem. But Naomi tried again:

Return home, my daughters. Why would you come
with me? Am I going to have any more sons, who
could become your husbands? Return home, my
daughters; I am too old to have another husband.
Even if I thought there was still hope for me—even
if I had a husband tonight and then gave birth to
sons— would you wait until they grew up? Would
you remain unmarried for them? No, my daughters.
It is more bitter for me than for you, because the
Lord's hand has gone out against me! (1:11-13).

What is the tone of Naomi's argument to Orpah
and Ruth? It isn't just another effort to persuade
them not to stay with her. It is also a lament accusing God of botching up her life. It affirms God's
direct involvement in her life and His accountability
for her situation. Basically Naomi told Orpah and
Ruth that if God was "after" her, to stay with her was
to court disaster.

The second effort to persuade them had its
effect on Orpah, who kissed her mother-in-law
and started back to Moab. But Ruth still wasn't
persuaded. In the next verses we hear her unshak-
able decision to stay with Naomi:

Don't urge me to leave you or to turn back from
you. Where you go, I will go, and where you
stay I will stay. Your people will be my people
and your God my God. Where you die I will die,
and there I will be buried. May the Lord deal with
me, be it ever so severely, if anything but death
separates you and me (1:16-17).

With that Naomi gave up trying to talk Ruth into returning to Moab.

Can we fault Orpah for going back to Moab? Not at all. Orpah did the expected thing. It is Ruth who did the unexpected. We understand the reasonableness of Orpah's decision. We don't understand the incredible loyalty Ruth displayed. Ruth demonstrated what the Hebrews called *hesed*.

Hesed is a Hebrew word we can translate "loyal love." It is a love that goes well beyond the expected. David's mighty men showed *hesed* for their beloved leader a hundred years later when they left the wilderness and fought their way into and out of Bethlehem to bring David a drink of water from the town well. God shows us *hesed* in sacrificing even His own Son to redeem us, to buy us back from sin. Ruth was a shining example of *hesed* as she stood at a crossroad between familiar Moab and unfamiliar Judah.

Her loyal love made the choice—for Naomi's people and for Naomi's God. We see her making that choice with no husband and no prospect of marriage, devoting herself to an old woman. She might have wished for a crystal ball as she stood on that dusty road so many years ago. It would have been nice to see how her choice would work out. But she had none. She had to choose for God and Naomi with no guarantees.

The scene continues. In verse 19 we see the two women arriving in Bethlehem where everyone came out to greet them. "Can this be Naomi?" It had been more than ten years since she had left. Suddenly hearing her name, *Naomi,* the old woman was reminded of the irony of that name. Naomi means "pleasant" or "lovely." "Lovely?" she exclaimed. "Don't call me Naomi [Lovely] . . . . Call me Mara [Bitter]" (1:20).

As Naomi continued speaking, her anger at God spilled over once again.

> *The Almighty has made my life very bitter. I went away full, but the Lord has brought me back empty* (1:20-21).

Throughout this first act we hear Naomi talking about God. She was conscious of His work in the universe and in her life. But as she talked about God, we see that she misjudged Him and she misjudged life. She stated that she went out of Judah full. But did she? The very thing that caused her family's migration to Moab was a famine. They went out empty. Life was tough or they would not have left Bethlehem in the first place.

Naomi also stated that God had brought her back empty. But had He? It was true that she had lost her husband and both sons. But in their place God had given her the incredible devotion of Ruth, who pledged to stay with her to death's door and beyond.

Naomi misjudged her situation when she misjudged God. She focused on the negative and became bitter. Calling herself "Mara" (bitter), she looked at God and looked at life through dirty windows.

Like Naomi, we can be religious. We can talk about God. We can offer prayers to God. But if we misjudge Him and His work in our lives, we easily misjudge all that touches us.

As act one and chapter one end, the curtain slowly descends on two women: loyal Ruth and bitter Naomi. The last words of the last verse of this chapter give us a clue to what is to follow in the next act. Ruth and Naomi had arrived in Bethlehem as the barley harvest began. What did this presage for two poor widows newly arrived in town?

Act Two. As the curtain rises on act two, we discover that Naomi had a relative in town who was wealthy and influential. Was he destined for some crucial role in our play?

Meanwhile, Naomi and Ruth had nothing to eat. Ruth decided to glean, that is to follow the reapers during the harvest and to pick up from the ground any grains left behind. In this act, Naomi moves to the stage wing and Ruth moves to center stage.

In Ruth 2:3 we read that "as it turned out, she found herself working in a field belonging to Boaz." That statement makes it sound as if all that followed was purely accidental. But the author is actually hinting at a cause for this "chance" happening. Behind what appears to be human luck lies divine purpose. Even in the "accidents" in life, the hand of God is at work on our behalf.

Now look at verse 4:

"Just then Boaz arrived from Bethlehem."

Surprise! One more coincidence! The wealthy, influential relative of Naomi owned the field and happened on the scene while Ruth was there!

Noticing Ruth, he asked about her and learned that she was from Moab and had come back with Naomi. Now comes the moment of truth. "Chance" had thrown Ruth and Boaz together in the same field. What would Boaz do?

Obviously, things are turning out well. Boaz, in short, gives Ruth "most favored gleaner" status in his fields. By following his instructions carefully, Ruth would be protected from young men who might try to bother her. She would also glean much more grain than would normally be the case.

Not only did Boaz make Ruth's gleaning easier, but he also invited her to eat with his harvesters and saw to it that she had an adequate meal. At the end of her first day of gleaning, she returned to Naomi with a shawl full of winnowed grain. The Bible tells us that she took home an ephah of barley—about twenty-nine pounds of grain. Ruth's success on her first day of gleaning far exceeded her expectations when she set out that morning.

What happened when she returned to Naomi that evening? Of course, the older woman wanted a full recounting of all that had happened that day.

Such a huge shawl-full of grain meant that she had gleaned in a good place. Where had she gone? In whose field had she gleaned?

Notice Naomi's reaction when Ruth answered her questions. Hearing about Boaz, she exclaimed, "The Lord bless him! . . . That man is our close relative; he is one of our kinsman-redeemers" (2:20).

What does that mean? Why is that important? The curtain descends slowly on our second act. But Naomi's statement about a kinsman-redeemer lets us know that the play is not over.

Act Three. Act three is about to begin. It turns out to be the turning point in the play. God has provided food for the two widows. But that is only a short-term solution to their needs. Ruth needs a husband. Naomi needs a son to preserve her inheritance and to carry on the family name. As the barley and wheat harvests end, Naomi cooks up a scheme that is bold, brash, and a little bit dangerous for Ruth. Read her plan in 3:1-4.

> One day Naomi her mother-in-law said to her, "My daughter, should I not try to find a home for you, where you will be well provided for? Is not Boaz, with whose servant girls you have been, a kinsman of ours? Tonight he will be winnowing barley on the threshing floor. Wash and perfume yourself, and put on your best clothes. Then go down to the threshing floor, but don't let him know you are there until he has finished eating and drinking. When he lies

*down, note the place where he is lying. Then go
and uncover his feet and lie down. He will tell
you what to do."*

Thus Naomi began to answer her own prayer for
Ruth back in Ruth 1:9—"May the Lord grant that
each of you will find rest in the home of another
husband." In one way Naomi models for us the way
God works through human actions. We are not
to wait passively for events to happen. When an
opportunity presents itself, we may need to seize the
initiative. Naomi did just that. But we also recognize
that in Naomi's plan lay real risk for Ruth.

Boaz and Ruth would be in a secluded spot
where they could talk privately. In Old Testament
times, however, threshing floors were associated
with licentiousness. Naomi was gambling on the
character of Boaz, that he would not take unfair
advantage of Ruth. Naomi was asking Ruth to enter
an uncertain, compromising situation with a great
deal hanging in the balance.

What was hanging in the balance? Was Ruth
being asked to seduce Boaz there on the threshing
floor?

The Levirate Law required that if a man died
without an heir, his brother was to marry the
widow. The first son born to them then became
the legal heir of the deceased husband and continued his name, inheriting his property. If no brother
were available to marry the widow, she could ask
a more distant relative to do so. Here we see Ruth

using a strange old custom to propose marriage to Boaz. The meaning of what she did was to ask for Boaz's total protection.

I've always been glad for many reasons that I was born a female. One reason is that as a woman in our culture, I never had to risk rejection by having to propose marriage to a man! But Ruth lived in a different time and place. She had to take that risk.

She didn't propose as someone might today. Rather, she asked Boaz to spread his garment over her as a kinsman-redeemer. That act symbolized his intention to protect her. It was like giving and receiving an engagement ring today.

Did he do it? Yes and no. He replied, "Mmmm, yes. I'd like to do that. But I'm not your nearest kinsman-redeemer. There is another man who is closer to Naomi by family ties. He has first choice. It's up to him" (see 3:12-13).

So, no. They were not engaged that night. But Ruth knew that Boaz would marry her if the nearer kinsman reneged. Boaz would settle things properly and leave the outcome to God.

Ruth remained quietly at Boaz's feet throughout the night, then just as quietly went back to Bethlehem before dawn. The curtain descends on our third act as Ruth tells Naomi everything that happened.

Even the schemes of men and women can be used by God to accomplish His purposes. This scheme did not turn sour, not because the circumstances were not right for hanky-panky, but because of the character of Ruth and Boaz. Boaz was concerned for Ruth's reputation. She was safe. Naomi staked the scheme on Boaz's integrity. He proved to be a man of honor. But the question now in the air is, Which guy will get the girl?

Act Four. The curtain rises on act four. We see Boaz at the city gate, where he knew he would find the nearer kinsman. It was certain that Ruth would soon have a husband. What was not certain was who it would be. What up to this point had been a private matter between Naomi, Ruth, and Boaz now had to become public. This was a family matter to be worked out between the kinsmen in a public meeting.

Assembling ten witnesses, Boaz addressed the nearer kinsman about redeeming the property of Elimelech. The kinsman must have thought, Sure. That looks easy enough, so he replied, "I will redeem it" (4:4). He knew he would have to marry the widow to do that, but he assumed that Naomi was too old to have children and he would end up with the property with no heir to claim it. Financially the investment was a bargain without risk. How could he lose?

Boaz sprang the clincher: Ruth comes with the property. If the nearer kinsman bought it, he bought her as well. The kinsman would be obliged to father a son by Ruth to perpetuate Elimelech's name over his inheritance. In other words, the kinsman would not be allowed to keep the property when the son was old enough to claim his inheritance.

Suddenly the picture changed for the nearer kinsman. He quickly waived his prior rights of redemption. Boaz would get Ruth! The crowd cheered and Boaz took his bride home.

What follows in this act ties up all the loose ends in our story. It isn't enough that the guy gets the girl or the girl gets the guy. All of that is for a larger purpose.

One purpose lies in perpetuating Elimelech's name over his inheritance. For that, Naomi must have a son. But she's too old for that! Not by Jewish law. When her kinsman Boaz and Ruth, her daughter-in-law, produce a son, we see an interesting procession winding through the streets of Bethlehem. The women of the town are carrying this tiny baby and placing him in the arms of Naomi. Naomi now has a son. The bitter woman who complained in the first act about being empty is now full. Not only is she well-fed but she also has a son to carry on her husband's name. This son is Elimelech's legal heir.

Does our story end here? No. We still have that strange genealogy as the climax of our story. What do we learn from it? Pick up reading where I left off (on page 46): "Salmon the father of Boaz, Boaz the father of Obed, Obed the father of Jesse, and Jesse the father of David" (4:21-22).

David! Suddenly the simple, clever human story of two struggling widows takes on a new dimension. This bitter old woman and this foreign Moabitess become bright threads woven into the fabric of Israel's national history.

God provided bread through Ruth's gleaning. God provided security through Ruth's marriage to Boaz. God provided posterity for Elimelech and Naomi. Even more, God provided a great king for the nation Israel through a foreign woman. God used the faithfulness of ordinary people to accomplish great things.

We find the same genealogy in Matthew 1:3-6.

Perez the father of Hezron, Hezron the father of Ram, Ram the father of Amminadab, Amminadab the father of Nahshon, Nahshon the father of Salmon, Salmon the father of Boaz, whose mother was Rahab, Boaz the father of Obed, whose mother was Ruth, Obed the father of Jesse, and Jesse the father of King David.

This genealogy does not stop with David. After many more unpronounceable names, we read in verse 16:

. . . and Jacob the father of Joseph, the husband of Mary, of whom was born Jesus, who is called Christ.

Not only did the faithful Ruth and the upright Boaz serve as great-grandparents of Israel's greatest king but they also stand in the line of those through whom God chose to send His Son into the world to bring us salvation.

Many times on a dreary Tuesday afternoon we may find it hard to believe that God is really at work in our lives. God seems hidden from us. Like Naomi in the first act, we can misjudge life because we are not sure God is actively involved in our lives.

Things happen that look like accidents—like Ruth gleaning in the fields of Boaz. Life can seem haphazard and accidental. But over all the seeming accidents in our lives God is at work, making divine appointments with us through the things that happen to us. God is the Stage Manager in control of all the players on the stage. In the midst of what seems terribly ordinary, He is doing something extraordinary.

It has been said that what we are determines what we see. We may look for God and miss Him because we confuse Him with shining angels. God is found not just in the miraculous and the extraordinary. He is at work in us and through us in the dailiness of life. On a dreary Tuesday afternoon we can get the idea that life is all up to us. But if we belong to God, even when we don't see Him at work, we

> *God provided a great king for the nation Israel through a foreign woman.*

can be sure that God is moving events on our behalf.

Ruth made a choice on a dusty road between Moab and Bethlehem. She chose to give her loyalty to God and His people. That choice may have seemed insignificant, but it changed Naomi and it changed history.

When you and I choose God and His people, we may hear no bells ringing. But the silence does not mean the choice is not life-changing. As Christians, we are involved in an incredible drama. There are no ordinary days. There are no insignificant choices. If we saw our life as God sees it, we'd be overwhelmed. On a dreary Tuesday afternoon we can remind ourselves that as we choose for God and His people, God will use that choice in ways that exceed our imagination.

HANNAH:
How To Deal With Depression

DEPRESSION. It happens to the best of people. In her book *Some Run With Feet Of Clay*, actress Jeannette Clift tells of a conversation she had with a good friend:

> The other day I called one of the most productive Christians I know. "How are you," I asked, thinking it was a somewhat needless question. She was always fine, and had nineteen Scripture verses to prove it! I didn't get her usual answer, though. Instead I got a long pause, and then words all capsulated in one breath. "Oh, Jeannette, I'm awful! I've been so depressed I don't know what to do. I've had to quit teaching my Bible classes. I'm not doing anything. I don't go out, I don't see anybody. It's all I can do just to get up in the morning, and some days I can't even do that.

I'm so ashamed of myself I don't think I can stand it!"

Jeannette explains:

> This was no erratic spiritual novice; this was a mighty Christian soldier! I had seen her in action and praised God for her accuracy as she taught or counseled. My heart hurt for her. This dear friend was not only down in the depths, but ashamed of herself for being there .... Any Christian who is truly shocked by another Christian's depression has not dealt honestly with the possibility of her own.

In the past year, I have spent many hours with each of two close friends trapped in the web of paralyzing depression. One woman is the college friend whose faith and commitment to Christ brought me into a personal relationship with God. She and her husband have ministered effectively in Christ's name in East Africa for more than thirty years. During this furlough, however, she has been plunged into severe depression.

My second friend was a colleague in ministry in France. Gifted with a splendid mind, she has not always found doors open to the use of her gifts. Focusing her energies on her family, she and her husband have successfully parented two model sons. Now that the boys are grown, she has not been able to find outlets for all that she has to give. She has lived for several years now in a miasma of depression.

Cynthia Swindoll, former executive director of the radio ministry Insight For Living, looked back over the fifteen years in which her life was darkened by depression. In the preface to Don Baker's book, *Depression*, she described her experience:

> [It was] black as a thousand midnights in a cypress swamp. [It was] loneliness that is indescribable. [It brought] confusion regarding God. [I experienced] frustration with life and circumstances. [It was] the feeling that you have been abandoned, that you are worthless. [I felt] unlovable. The pain was excruciating.

Depression. Did you notice the feelings Cynthia Swindoll had? She felt lonely, confused, frustrated, worthless, unlovable. The pain, she said, was excruciating.

Depression comes in many forms with many symptoms. Perhaps you experience some of them right now. Dr. Timothy Foster lists seven main symptoms of depression in his helpful book *How To Deal With Depression.*

1. We lose emotional feeling and call it "the blahs." This is that drop in mood in which we say, "I don't feel particularly bad; I don't feel particularly good. I just don't feel much of anything." (Foster reminds us that every emotionally caused depression starts with a case of the blahs that hangs on and gradually deteriorates.)

2. *We become overly self-conscious.* Most of the time we do scores of things "on automatic pilot"— we drive the car, cross our legs, scratch our noses, or eat dinner with no conscious thought about our actions. But suddenly we have to think about what are usually unconscious decisions. We become self-conscious.

3. *Our sleep patterns change.* If we normally sleep through the night, we may experience sleeplessness. If we usually function well on 7 or 8 hours of sleep at night, we may find that we want to sleep all the time.

4. *Our eating patterns change.* If we have always kept our weight under control with disciplined eating, we may find ourselves reaching for food constantly. Or we may lose our normal appetite and cannot force ourselves to eat.

5. *Our crying patterns change.* This too can take two forms. If we cry regularly, we may find something holding back normal tears. We can't cry. Something blocks the flow of our emotions. Or we may constantly feel that we need to cry. The tears are always only an inch below the surface.

6. *We lose confidence in our ability to function.* With this we may experience a loss of energy or a lack of initiative.

7. *Our mood drops.* We feel sad. Depression often starts with feeling "nothing" or the blahs, but eventually the mood drops and a combination of sadness and not caring sets in.

Foster states that the presence of only one or two of these symptoms should not alarm us. But if we experience three or more of these symptoms, we may be in depression.

Where does depression come from? In most cases it can be traced to the way we think about ourselves.

Some depressions—about five percent of them —are due to a biochemical imbalance and must be treated with medications for life. It is estimated that the other ninety-five percent of depressions are rooted in emotional factors.

Depression is one way of handling stress. Some people handle stress by becoming physically ill. Others might handle stress by over-achieving. Still others handle stress with a drop in mood—by checking out from participation in life.

> *Stress often moves in with us when we focus on ourselves.*

Many depressions are caused by some trau-matic event in our lives. We can point to those events and explain why we are depressed. Perhaps we feel rejected by someone we value. Or we've just come through a devastating divorce. Or perhaps someone close to us has recently died. Maybe it's a job loss with the threat of losing our house. Depression from loss is the easiest kind to understand.

Other depressions can't be tied to anything spe-cific that has happened to us. We feel down "for no reason at all."

Stress often moves in with us when we focus

on ourselves negatively. It comes when we feel powerless to change our situation. We see no alternatives from which to choose. Wherever we turn, we see closed doors or roadblocks shutting us off from happiness. What is merely a minor barrier for one person becomes an insurmountable obstacle for another.

For many people in their middle years, depression comes when they realize that they will never become what once they dreamed of being. Psychologists call this *involutional melancholia*. Helplessness gradually becomes both a cause and an effect of depression.

All depressed people experience a decrease in self-confidence. If I have low self-esteem, I am much more vulnerable to depression. Something happens to me that confirms my idea that I'm no good. The scenario might look like this:

I'm a professor at Gordon-Conwell Theological Seminary. Suppose the department head stops by my office and asks me if I have finished a project he gave me to do. I haven't. So I feel his disappointment in me. I begin to translate that into all kinds of feelings he, in reality, isn't having. If my self-esteem is low, I may conclude that he is disgusted with me for not getting my work done. In fact, I assume, he is getting so disgusted that he will probably fire me. I believe that I deserve whatever he throws at me because I am not a capable person. I am really a failure. Because I am so worthless and really am a handicap to my students, the best thing I can do is to quit my job so my boss can hire someone else who will do the job correctly.

Have you ever played that kind of scenario in your head? I have. What happens is that I file this incident away in my memory where I have already filed many other incidents of "rejection." My level of self-confidence sinks a bit lower each time under the weight of this heavy file drawer full of my failures.

As my self-confidence drains away, I withdraw from people around me, from life in general, and often from God. I'm probably not conscious of my reasons for withdrawing. But the more I withdraw, the more I blame myself. This merely increases the problem. Each time I do this, my self-confidence hits a new low. A vicious cycle begins to spin, leading me into more withdrawal and more feelings of guilt and worthlessness.

Caught in the cycle, I feel totally helpless. Nothing that I do is worth anything. I'm at the mercy of forces that overwhelm me in my inadequacy. I feel myself being sucked down, down in a spiraling whirlpool of depression.

Negative thoughts about ourselves quickly become automatic. We don't have to work at thinking negative thoughts. They become well-ingrained habits strengthened by years of practice. We do not arrive at negative thoughts through logic. We reach most of them with no objective evidence at all. But that doesn't stop us.

Depression creates a frame of mind in which almost everything we experience reminds us of our miserable, helpless condition. This is one reason depression is so painful. We really believe we are to blame for whatever we think is wrong. We hold ourselves responsible for everything bad that happens around us. We emphasize failures and we ignore successes or brush them aside as accidental.

Most of the time, depressed people anchor their sense of self-worth to a very narrow idea of what success is. Unrealistic expectations and impossibly high goals lead us to an overwhelming sense of failure and worthlessness. We set ourselves up to fail. The mental habit of inflating others and deflating ourselves is typical of depression. We end up with distorted perceptions of other people that leave us feeling hopelessly inferior. We see ourselves as stupid, unattractive, untalented, or unspiritual.

> *Depression creates a frame of mind in which almost everything we experience reminds us of our miserable, helpless condition.*

So much for a clinical description of depression. It can be helpful to review symptoms and the syndrome. But this isn't a medical journal and depression is not a virus. It is always personal. It happens to real people. We may understand it better if we look at a biblical case study in depression.

Our case study is a woman named Hannah. Her story can help us as we walk with her through and out of her depression. We meet her in 1 Samuel 1. As we get acquainted with her, we discover that she had several sources of stress.

First, she lived at a stressful time in Israel's history. The nation was merely a loose confederacy of tribes united around the worship of Jehovah at the shrine at Shiloh. Invaders harassed one tribe, then another. Over a period of several hundred years one or another strong leader called a judge would deliver God's people from foreign rule, only to find another Israelite tribe oppressed by a different group of outsiders.

As we flip on the news or pick up *Time* or *Newsweek*, we can understand how the tensions in the world and in our town can affect the way we feel. Not only was Hannah's nation oppressed by neighbor nations but also the religious life of the people was being corrupted by bad priests. The two sons of the high priest made a mockery of the sacrifices, and to make bad matters worse, they were sleeping with the women who served at the entrance to the tabernacle. It was not a time to inspire faith and devotion to God.

Yet, in the midst of religious hypocrisy we find a pious family in Ramah in the hill country allotted to the tribe of Ephraim. Elkanah, the husband in our story, was a Levite, or a priest. Every year he and his family made the ten-mile journey on foot to the tabernacle or shrine at Shiloh to worship.

Hannah lived at a stressful time both politically and religiously. But she also had to live with stress in her family. In 1 Samuel 1:2 we learn that Elkanah had two wives—Hannah, who was beloved but barren, and Peninnah, who was less loved but very fertile. Some of Hannah's stress came from living in a polygamous marriage.

Polygamy was a fact of life in ancient Israel. Wives were a means of securing children. In Hannah's case it is likely that she was Elkanah's first wife. But because she was infertile, he took a second wife to insure that the family name would not be lost because he had no children.

In Hannah's day, a woman who failed to produce children was considered to be a useless link in the chain leading to the promised Messiah. Hannah's situation was depressing. Year after year Peninnah produced children. Year after year Hannah suffered emotionally from her infertility, her hopes for a pregnancy receding as each month went by. Hannah's stress in the family came not just from being in a polygamous marriage. It also came from her infertility as she lived next to a co-wife who had no trouble conceiving and bearing children.

Hannah's stress, however, was compounded by the fact that Peninnah never stopped needling her about her childlessness. In verse 6 we read that her rival, Peninnah, "kept provoking her in order to irritate her." We know from verse 7 that this had been going on for a long time—"year after year."

One of the most trying times for Hannah appears to have been the annual pilgrimage to Shiloh. Imagine having to walk for ten miles with someone who never stops picking at your inadequacy all the while her children keep bumping into you, wiping their noses on your skirt, or asking you to carry them. No wonder Hannah arrived at Shiloh under a black cloud of depression.

How do we know she was depressed? What were some of her symptoms? Elkanah's questions to his wife in verse 8 give us some clues:

Why are you weeping?

Why don't you eat?

Why are you downhearted?

Think back to Foster's seven major symptoms of depression (pp. 64-65). He said that any three indicated depression. Hannah was depressed. Elkanah's well-intentioned effort to console her did not succeed. Nothing seemed to make any difference. Her despair was overpowering. She withdrew from the comfort of her husband. She withdrew from the family circle.

If you have ever been in the black hole of depression, you can sympathize with Hannah. She was depressed, and she had much in her life to cause her depression. In the midst of it all, however, Hannah had not lost her grip on God. Watch what happens next. In verses 9 and 10 we read:

Once when they had finished eating and drinking in Shiloh, Hannah stood up. Now Eli the priest was sitting on a chair by the doorpost of the Lord's temple [tabernacle]. In bitterness of soul Hannah wept much and prayed to the Lord.

Note that while we have learned a lot about Hannah in the Bible story up to this point, we only now hear Hannah herself speak. We have had no indication whether she answered Peninnah's jeers or whether she tried to help Elkanah understand her misery when he attempted to console her. Until she speaks in verse 11, she has been a silent suffering figure, very much like many people suffering from depression today. Depression has a way of robbing us of the ability to communicate with the important people around us. We may feel that no one will understand.

In bitterness of soul she wept. But she did something else. She prayed to the Lord. The first time we hear her speak, we hear her addressing God:

She made a vow, saying, "O LORD Almighty, if you will only look upon your servant's misery and remember me, and not forget your servant but give her a son, then I will give him to the LORD for all the days of his life, and no razor will ever be used on his head" (v. 11).

Hannah's vow was called a Nazirite vow. Samson, an earlier judge of Israel, was also a Nazirite, "set apart to God from birth," one who would "begin the deliverance of Israel from the hands of the Philistines" (Judges 13:5). Jews believed that anything that had not been touched, plowed, or cut belonged to the Lord. A field was the Lord's until it was plowed. Once a farmer dug it up, it was his and not the Lord's. A person dedicated to the Lord from his birth could not have his hair cut. Once it was cut, he no longer had the same relationship to the Lord. This explains what happened to Samson when Delilah wheedled the secret of his strength from him, and a razor was used on his head.

Listen to Hannah as she bargained for a son. Feel her desperation and the urgency of her petition. "Look at my misery! Remember me! Don't forget me! Give me a son!" We hear the heaviness in the words she prays. We see it in the way she prays. Read 1 Samuel 1: 12-16:

> As she kept on praying to the LORD, Eli observed her mouth. Hannah was praying in her heart, and her lips were moving but her voice was not heard. Eli thought she was drunk and said to her, "How long will you keep on getting drunk? Get rid of your wine." "Not so, my lord," Hannah replied, "I am a woman who is deeply troubled. I have not been drinking wine or beer; I was pouring out my soul to the Lord. Do not take your servant for a wicked woman; I have been praying here out of my great anguish and grief."

Added to Peninnah's jibes and Elkanah's ineffective effort at consolation came a sharp rebuke from the high priest. In the midst of her misery, Hannah also had to deal with unjustified criticism from one who misunderstood her.

In the prayer in verse 11 she made a vow that if the Lord gave her the desire of her heart, she would give that son back to Him to serve Him all the days of his life. But that vow and her pleas do not account for all the time Hannah stood praying. In verse 10 we read that "in bitterness of soul Hannah wept much and prayed," and in verse 12, "she kept on praying."

Sympathetic to Hannah's words, Eli told her in verse 17 to "go in peace, and may the God of Israel grant you what you have asked of him." Notice that Eli did not know what Hannah had asked God to do. He merely added his prayer to hers to the God of Israel. Yet something happened to Hannah as she stood there praying. Whatever it was, it produced the result we see in verse 18:

> *Then she went her way and ate something, and her face was no longer downcast.*

Hannah joined in the worship of the Lord the next morning, went back to Ramah with Elkanah, and voila!—before long she was pregnant and gave birth to Samuel, whose name means "heard of God." She asked, and God heard her and answered her prayer. No wonder her depression lifted! She had the baby she asked for.

Is that really what happened? If our story ended with 1 Samuel chapter 1, we might think that the only way out of depression is to have God intervene in some miraculous way to fill up the empty places in our lives. But the story doesn't end with chapter 1. The key to understanding Hannah's dramatic turnaround in verse 18 lies in her song, or psalm, that we find in 1 Samuel 2:1-10.

Hannah's depression lifted when she took her focus from herself and her situation and put her focus on God. In the midst of her misery she was able to focus on three important facts about God. She underlined these three facts in her song.

The first thing she knew about God is found in 1 Samuel 2:2,

There is no one holy like the LORD; there is no one besides you; there is no Rock like our God.

She recognized God's holiness. What could the fact of God's holiness mean to a woman in depression? Far from being consoling, that could only intensify the feelings of worthlessness and guilt that are often part of depression.

If we define holiness negatively—as a separation from all that is unclean—that may make us feel worse about ourselves. But God's holiness is much more.

Charles Ryrie suggests an analogy that may help us understand this word *holy*. Ryrie asks, "What does it mean to be healthy?" It means the absence of illness. But we all know that being healthy is a lot more than simply not being sick. It also means having energy, being physically able to meet the demands of our daily lives.

Holiness is not merely the absence of evil. It is also the presence of positive right. It is God at work doing what is positively right for us. It is the part of God's nature that keeps Him from doing anything in our lives that is not in our best interest.

His love is a holy and pure love that is committed to our best good.

The second thing Hannah knew about God is found in 1 Samuel 2:3,

> For the LORD is a God who knows, and by him deeds are weighed.

The New American Standard Bible translates this verse, "For the Lord is a God of knowledge." Not only does God's holiness keep Him committed to our best good but His perfect knowledge also keeps Him from doing anything in our lives that is not perfectly right for us.

Someone has said that "God does not waste His strokes in our lives." That is true. It is true because God knows what is best for us. No trial and error. No foul balls or strikeouts. The Lord is a God of knowledge. That gives us confidence in His actions in our lives.

The third thing Hannah knew occupies much of her song. God has power. We see this in 1 Samuel 2:6-7 and at the end of verse 8:

> The LORD brings death and makes alive; he brings down to the grave and raises up. The LORD sends poverty and wealth; he humbles and he exalts.
> . . . For the foundations of the earth are the LORD's; upon them he has set the world.

The Lord of creation has all power. He can do whatever He wants to do. That fact without the first two facts might terrify us. If God had all power and we did not know anything else about Him, we would have reason for a massive depression. We would all cower in dark corners to escape His wrath or His caprice. But God tempers His power with His commitment to our welfare. He controls His power with His knowledge of what is best for us.

My husband, Randy, and I have four adult children. We have always wanted the best for our children. But often we didn't know what was best for them. Which schools would be best? Which activities would be most wholesome? Which church would nurture them? As our children grew up, we made thousands of decisions with their interests at heart. But we were not always sure that our choices were wise.

Not only have Randy and I often lacked knowledge of what was best for our children; there were times when we knew what was best but didn't have the power to make that decision stick. We're finite, fallible parents who have made lots of mistakes along the way. We wanted what was best for our children, but we lacked the knowledge and the power we needed.

God is not finite. God is not fallible. He not only wants what is best for us and knows with perfect knowledge what is best but He also has the power to make the best happen in our lives. God's holy commitment to us, God's knowledge of what is best for us, and God's power to make the right things happen in our lives are all linked together for our good.

What brought Hannah out of her depression? She saw God as He really is. God backed His commitment to her welfare with His knowledge and His power to do what needed to be done in her life.

Hannah's story had a happy ending. Samuel was born. She gave him to the Lord, and God gave her three more sons and two daughters. Yet in 1 Samuel 1:18, when she stopped praying, ate some food, and stopped looking sad, she didn't know at that moment how the story would end. She was able to do that because she had met with God and understood who He was and what He could do.

At the beginning of this section, I mentioned that psychologists believe depression is related to the way we think about ourselves. It is also true that depression is related to the way we think—or fail to think—about God. Once we bind ourselves to a God-sized God, we have a resource for dealing with depression. We can focus on God—His holiness, His knowledge, His power. We can face our fears and anxieties in the light of His character and His commitment to us.

If depression results from the way we think about ourselves, then it can be lifted by the way we think about ourselves in relation to a holy, knowledgeable, and powerful God who is committed to us.

Robert Browning reminds us that " 'tis looking downward that makes one dizzy." I'm an acrophobe. I don't like being up high on the top of things like fire towers or monuments or skyscrapers. Looking down terrifies me.

Spiritually speaking, the downward look is the one that leads to depression. The upward look takes away our fear. Look to the God of Hannah, the One who dispelled her depression with a new understanding of His love, His knowledge, and His power.

This chapter is excerpted from A Woman God Can Lead *by Alice Mathews, published by Discovery House Publishers* © *1998.*

Three

DAVID & MANASSEH

Overcoming Failure

ver the years I have learned that God has many ways to make us into the people He wants us to be. But it seems that His preferred method is through resistance. The greater the resistance, the greater the growth. What we see as obstacles to achievement, God sees as opportunities for growth. Disappointment, loss, criticism, failure, humiliation, temptation, depression, loneliness, and moral failure become the means by which we grow strong if we are "trained" by these forces, as the author of Hebrews would say (12:11).

This chapter is mainly about overcoming failure. We will examine two Old Testament men who failed miserably, David and Manasseh, and see how God used their failure to make them strong. We will discover that God wastes nothing in our lives—not even sin.

— *David Roper*

MANASSEH:
Overcoming A Bad Start

I T WAS NEW YEAR'S DAY, 1929. The University of California at Berkeley was playing Georgia Tech in the Rose Bowl. Roy Riegels, a Cal defensive back, recovered a Georgia Tech fumble, ran laterally across the field, turned, and then scampered sixty-five yards in the wrong direction—straight toward Cal's goal line. One of his own players tackled Riegels just before he would have scored for Georgia Tech. On the next play, Georgia Tech blocked the punt and scored.

From that day on, Riegels was saddled with the infamous name, "Wrong-way Riegels." For years afterward whenever he was introduced, people would exclaim, "Oh, yeah. I know who you are! You're the guy who ran the wrong way in the Rose Bowl!"

It may be that our failures are not as conspicuous as Riegels' was, but we have our own alternate routes and wrongway runs. And we have the memories that accompany them—recollections that rise up to taunt us and haunt us at three o'clock in the morning. There's so much of our past we wish we could undo or redo—so much we wish we could forget. If only we could begin again.

Louisa Fletcher Tarkington wrote for all of us when she mused:

> I wish that there were some wonderful place
> called the Land of Beginning Again,
> Where all our mistakes, and all our heart-
> aches, and all of our poor selfish griefs could
> be dropped like a shabby old coat at the
> door, and never be put on again.

There is such a place. It is found in the grace of God—a grace that not only completely forgives our past and puts it away, but also uses it to make us better than ever before. "Even from sin," Augustine said, "God can draw good."

■ MANASSEH'S GODLY HERITAGE

Manasseh was the son of Hezekiah, one of the few kings of Judah who "did what was right in the eyes of the Lord" (2 Kings 18:3). Israel's historian tells us:

> *[Hezekiah] removed the high places, smashed the sacred stones, and cut down the Asherah poles. He broke into pieces the bronze snake Moses had made, for up to that time the Israelites had been burning incense to it. (It was called Nehushtan.) Hezekiah trusted in the Lord, the God of Israel. There was no one like him among all the kings of Judah, either before him or after him. He held fast to the LORD and did not cease to follow him;*

he kept the commands the LORD had given Moses
(2 Kings 18:4-6).

Hezekiah was responsible for a historic spiritual revival that rejuvenated Judah. He did away with the idols that his father, Ahaz, had worshiped, and he delivered his people from apostasy. He was helped greatly in his work of reformation by the prophetic ministries of Isaiah and Micah.

Hezekiah's son Manasseh ascended to the throne when he was twelve years old and reigned for ten years as coregent with his father. When he was twenty-two, his father died and the young king took over the reins of government. He reigned fifty-five years—from 697 to 642 BC—the longest rule in the history of both Judah and Israel.

Manasseh was blessed with a godly father. He lived through a time of spiritual vitality and prosperity. He was tutored by the prophets Isaiah and Micah. And he saw the Lord miraculously deliver Jerusalem while under siege by the Assyrians (2 Kings 19:35). Yet he didn't follow in his father's footsteps.

■ MANASSEH'S FAILURE OF LEADERSHIP

Scripture tells us that Manasseh "did evil in the eyes of the Lord, following the detestable practices of the nations the Lord had driven out before the Israelites" (2 Kings 21:2).

The "nations" of whom the author writes were the depraved and disgusting Canaanites.

Manasseh outdid them in his insane frenzy to break every rule—a madness spelled out in the following verses:

> He rebuilt the high places his father Hezekiah had destroyed; he also erected altars to Baal and made an Asherah pole, as Ahab king of Israel had done. He bowed down to all the starry hosts and worshiped them. He built altars in the temple of the LORD, of which the LORD had said, "In Jerusalem I will put my Name." In both courts of the temple of the LORD, he built altars to all the starry hosts. He sacrificed his own son in the fire, practiced sorcery and divination, and consulted mediums and spiritists. He did much evil in the eyes of the LORD, provoking Him to anger. He took the carved Asherah pole he had made and put it in the temple . . . . Manasseh led [the Israelites] astray, so that they did more evil than the nations the Lord had destroyed before the Israelites (2 Kings 21:3-7,9).

Manasseh's sins are recited here in an ascending order of deviance. First he "rebuilt the high places his father Hezekiah had destroyed." Ahaz, Manasseh's grandfather, had established "high places"—groves on the top of hills where the Asherah was worshiped. Hezekiah had torn them down (2 Kings 18:4). Manasseh built them up again.

Then Manasseh "erected altars to Baal," the chief Canaanite deity, and he made an Asherah pole as Ahab and Jezebel, Israel's diabolical duo, had done (1 Kings 16:33). The Asherah were images of a female deity, the consort of Baal, who represented the Canaanite goddess of sex and fertility. The pillars erected in her honor were evidently some sort of phallic symbols.

Manasseh worshiped the hosts of heaven and served them. He practiced astrology, giving his devotion to the sun, the moon, the planets, and the stars (see also Jeremiah 8:2; 19:13). He built altars to astral deities in the temple in Jerusalem, where God had said, "I will put my Name."

He made his sons pass through the fire—child sacrifice. According to the chronicler, "He sacrificed his sons in the fire in the Valley of Ben Hinnom." He also "practiced sorcery, divination, and witchcraft, and consulted mediums and spiritists" (2 Chronicles 33:6). The Hebrew text suggests that he did more than consult them, he "appointed" them. In other words, he gave them court appointments and put them in his cabinet.

If this were not enough, this debauched monarch then "took the carved Asherah pole he had made and put it in the temple." He took the aforementioned pornographic post, dedicated to everything ugly and obscene, and set it up in the Holy of Holies in the Lord's temple.

Nowhere is there the slightest hint of the worship of Yahweh. Manasseh selected his pantheon from the cultures surrounding Israel—from the Amorites, the Canaanites, the Philistines, the Phoenicians —but there is not one reference to the God who had revealed Himself to Israel.

The historian concluded, "Manasseh led [the Isrealites] astray, so that they did more evil than the nations the Lord had destroyed before the Israelites" (2 Kings 21:9).

Understand what's being said here: Manasseh alone bore the responsibility for bringing an entire nation down. What a legacy to leave behind!

And that's not all. There is a footnote that is terrible in its implications:

Manasseh also shed so much innocent blood that he filled Jerusalem from end to end—besides the sin that he had caused Judah to commit, so that they did evil in the eyes of the LORD (2 Kings 21:16).

Manasseh silenced the prophets with terrifying fury. Josephus, the Jewish historian, reports that Manasseh "slew all the righteous men that were among the Hebrews, nor would he spare the prophets, for he every day slew some of them until Jerusalem was overflown with blood."

There is a longstanding Jewish tradition reported in the Talmud that Manasseh put his old teacher, Isaiah, in a log and sawed it in two. This is almost certainly the background of the statement in the book of Hebrews that at least one of God's heroes was "sawed in two" (Hebrews 11:37).

■ THE REST OF THE STORY

As for the other events of Manasseh's reign, and all he did, including the sin he committed, are they not written in the book of the annals of the kings of

Judah? Manasseh rested with his fathers and was buried in his palace garden, the garden of Uzza. And Amon his son succeeded him as king (2 Kings 21:17-18).

Here is an odd thing: Manasseh thumbed his nose at God for fifty-five years, indulged himself in every lustful passion, corrupted and ruined an entire nation, and God sat on His hands.

Or did He?

Normally, we see only one side of God—His longsuffering patience: "The Lord longs to be gracious" (Isaiah 30:18). But there is another side: His "strange work" of judgment.

The whole story is not told in the books of Kings. The purpose of 1 and 2 Kings is to trace the decline of Israel and Judah to the Babylonian exile and to supply the reasons for that exile. The stories are necessarily abridged. The writer dwells only on those facts that contribute to his theme. The account of Manasseh's reign is resumed and supplemented in 2 Chronicles 33. The purpose of the chronicler was different. His theme was the restoration of the Davidic throne. For this purpose he selected events that contributed to that motif and included a number of facts that are omitted in Kings.

The first nine verses of 2 Chronicles 33 are basically a rewrite of 2 Kings 21:1-9 with a few minor changes. Then a new story emerges:

The Lord spoke to Manasseh and his people, but they paid no attention (2 Chronicles 33:10).

God's judgment did not fall precipitously. It never does. Theologian John Piper says, "[God's] anger must be released by a stiff safety lock, but His mercy has a hair trigger." God loves us too much to let us go. He pursues us—even into our sin and guilt—and pleads with us to turn back.

An old Turkish proverb says that God has "feet of wool and hands of steel." We may not hear Him coming, but when He gets His hands on us we cannot wriggle away. The flip side of the promise "I will never leave you nor forsake you" (Joshua 1:5) is the pledge that He will never leave us alone. He will hound us, badger us, bother us, pester us, and heckle us until we give in. God has many ways to deliver us from sin: sometimes by a drawing we feel in our souls; sometimes by a word dropped by a friend; sometimes by an incident related; or sometimes by a book, a sermon, a chance meeting. In these ways God appeals to us to come back to Him.

I remember a student I met at Stanford University years ago. He was sitting on a bench in front of Memorial Church reading the *Stanford Daily*. I sat down next to him, and we began to talk. The conversation went well until it turned to the subject of his relationship with God.

He leaped to his feet with a curse and stalked away. Then he stopped and turned around. "Forgive me," he said. "I was raised in a Christian home. My parents are Presbyterian missionaries in Taiwan, but I've been running away from God all my life. Yet wherever I go someone wants to talk to me about God."

More than anything, God wants us to give in to His love. "Love surrounds us," George MacDonald said, "seeking the smallest crack by which it may enter in." God waits tirelessly and loves relentlessly. But if we will not have Him, He will let us have our way and let us reap the consequences of our resistance. But even this is for our good. It is the redemptive judgment of God. God knows that when the cold wind blows it may turn our head around.

> So the LORD brought against them the army commanders of the king of Assyria, who took Manasseh prisoner, put a hook in his nose, bound him with bronze shackles and took him to Babylon. In his distress he sought the favor of the LORD his God and humbled himself greatly before the God of his fathers. And when he prayed to Him, the LORD was moved by his entreaty and listened to his plea; so He brought him back to Jerusalem and to his kingdom. Then Manasseh knew that the Lord is God (2 Chronicles 33:11-12).

The Assyrian king mentioned here was probably Esarhaddon, the son of Sennacherib. Esarhaddon put a ring in Manasseh's nose, manacles on his hands and feet, and marched him off to Babylon, where for twelve years he languished in a dungeon. A ring in the nose was the Assyrian way of humiliating conquered kings, a custom clearly illustrated on Assyrian artifacts. What utter humiliation! What awful ruin! But all to bring Manasseh home to God.

■ THE WAY BACK

Recovery begins with shame. MacDonald wrote, "To be ashamed is a holy and blessed thing. Shame is shame only to those who want to appear, not those who want to be. Shame is shame only to those who want to pass their examination, not to those who would get to the heart of things. . . . To be humbly ashamed is to be plunged in the cleansing bath of truth." Humility and contrition are the keys to the heart of God. Those are the keys Manasseh used.

> *In his distress he sought the favor of the* LORD *his God and humbled himself greatly before the God of his fathers* (2 Chronicles 33:12).

Josephus said that Manasseh "esteemed himself to be the cause of it all." He accepted full responsibility for what he had done—no denial, no excuses, no justification, no blame-shifting, no special pleading. Then Manasseh "humbled himself greatly."

Our tendency to make excuses for ourselves comes from thinking that God will never take us back unless we can minimize or explain away our wrongdoing. But, as C. S. Lewis observed, "Real forgiveness means looking steadily at the sin, that sin that is left over without any excuse, after all allowances have been made, and seeing it in all its horror, dirt, meanness, and malice, and nevertheless being wholly reconciled to the one who has done it. That, and only that, is forgiveness; and that we can always have from [God]."

Manasseh was not forsaken. Despite Manasseh's monstrous wickedness, the Lord was still his God. Although anger swept across God's face, He never turned away His eyes.

■ UNDYING LOVE

In Harriet Beecher Stowe's *Uncle Tom's Cabin*, Tom laments, "I's wicked I is—mighty wicked. Anyhow I can't help it!" Sin is our nature. It's how we make our way through life—and we can't help it. Yet our repeated failures do not change God's fundamental disposition toward us. If it's our nature to sin, it's His nature to save. Without that understanding we could never survive our sin. It would only terrorize us and drive us away from God.

We'd have grounds for that terror if God had chosen us in the beginning because we were so wonderful. But since our original acceptance did not depend on anything in us, it cannot be undone by anything in us now. Nothing in us deserved His favor before our conversion; nothing in us merits its continuation.

God saved us because He determined to do so. He created us for Himself, and without that fellowship His heart aches in loneliness. That's why Christ suffered for us—"the righteous for the unrighteous, to bring [us] to God" (1 Peter 3:18). He will never give up. He loves us too much to give up. "He who began a good work in [us] will carry it on to completion" (Philippians 1:6).

We must accept God's full and free forgiveness, and then forget ourselves. That we are sinners is undeniably true. That we are forgiven sinners is undeniable as well. We must not dwell on our sinfulness. God's heart is open to us. We must take what forgiveness we need and get on with life.

■ ENDING WELL

There is more. God not only forgives our sin but He also uses it to make us better than ever before. Consider Manasseh. He was released from prison after twelve years and restored to his throne. Then he set out to strengthen his defenses:

> When [Manasseh] prayed to Him, the LORD was moved by his entreaty and listened to his plea; so he brought him back to Jerusalem and to his kingdom. Then Manasseh knew that the LORD is God. Afterward he rebuilt the outer wall of the City of David, west of the Gihon spring in the valley, as far as the entrance of the Fish Gate and encircling the hill of Ophel; he also made it much higher. He stationed military commanders in all the fortified cities in Judah. He got rid of the foreign gods and removed the image from the temple of the Lord, as well as all the altars he had built on the temple hill and in Jerusalem; and he threw them out of the city. Then he restored the altar of the LORD and sacrificed fellowship offerings and thank offerings

on it, and told Judah to serve the LORD, *the God of Israel* (2 Chronicles 33:13-16).

Manasseh destroyed his pagan gods and removed the terrible idol he had set up in the house of the Lord. He hated his idols with as much fervor as he had loved them before.

He repaired the altar of the Lord, which he had broken down. He sacrificed on it peace offerings and thank offerings to praise God for His deliverance. He used his power to reform his people rather than to corrupt them.

This is what John the Baptist described as "fruit in keeping with repentance" (Matthew 3:8). True repentance involves a fundamental change in our outlook and attitude. It is not mere sorrow over sin. It is a radical reversal of our thinking. It will manifest itself in a determined effort to strengthen ourselves in those areas where we are weak and where we have fallen before. There will be a fierce determination to guard ourselves against sin.

True repentance will mean staying away from the company of a man or woman whose influence corrupts us. It will mean staying out of situations in which we're inclined to stumble and fall. It will mean staying away from polluting influences in movies, books, magazines, and cyberspace. It will mean finding another person to hold us accountable when we travel—someone who will keep us honest when we're away from home. Whatever it means, our waywardness will have made us stronger and better than ever before. Even from our sin God can draw good.

God gave Manasseh twenty more years of rule. He got a fresh and better start, and he made the most of it. He became one of the greatest kings of Judah, and for twenty-two years was a glorious example to Israel of God's unimaginable grace. God will do the same for you.

■ WHAT'S IN A NAME?

Manasseh's name is taken from a Hebrew verb that means "to forget." That's the word God writes over Manasseh's past and ours—*forgotten*. "I will forgive [your] wickedness and will remember [your] sins no more" (Jeremiah 31:34). Oswald Chambers says, "God forgets away our sins."

Jeffrey Dahmer comes to mind when sin of unforgivable proportion is considered. Dahmer confessed to murdering seventeen young men, dismembering some, having sex with their corpses, and eating parts of their bodies.

The media exposure surrounding his crimes turned Dahmer into a national symbol of evil. After his bloody death at the Columbia Correctional Center in Wisconsin, everyone was convinced that he was going straight to hell. One columnist uttered a fervent plea to the powers of darkness: "Take Jeffrey Dahmer, please."

But as it turned out, Dahmer had begun attending Bible studies in prison. He subsequently made a public profession of faith in Jesus Christ and was baptized. He found forgiveness and peace. He was calm about his fate, even after an inmate attempted to slit his throat during a chapel service. If he was sincere, and it appears that he was, we will see him one day in heaven.

Odd, isn't it? But such is the grace of God.

■ POSTSCRIPT

During halftime of that Rose Bowl game in 1929, Riegels hid in a corner of the UCLA locker room with a towel over his head. His coach, Nibs Price, said nothing to him and very little to the team.

Three minutes before the second half he said quietly, "The team that started the first half will start the second half." Riegels called out, "I can't, coach; I can't go back in. I've humiliated the team, the school, myself. I can't go back in." "Get back in the game, Riegels," Price replied. "It's only half over."

What a coach! What a God!

DAVID:
Overcoming Lies Of Self-Protection

WHEN FAILING and succeeding are at issue, an incident in David's life comes to mind. It took place during a period when he and Saul were playing a deadly game of hide and seek. Saul, pursuing David and his band of men in the Judean wilderness, was bent on running him into the ground.

Saul was familiar with all David's haunts and hiding places. David could run but he knew he could not hide. He was weary and worn out. There seemed to be no end to his troubles.

The songs that are assigned to this period of David's life are sad songs. The overriding mood is one of dreary depression and despair.

Why, O LORD, *do you stand far off? Why do you hide yourself in times of trouble? (Psalm 10:1).*

How long, O LORD? *Will you forget me forever? How long will you hide your face from me? (Psalm 13:1).*

My God, my God, why have you forsaken me? Why are you so far from saving me, so far from the words of my groaning? (Psalm 22:1).

■ DAVID'S DANGEROUS DECISION

David had reached the end of his rope. He just couldn't take it anymore. So he thought to himself:

One of these days I will be destroyed by the hand of Saul. The best thing I can do is to escape to the land of the Philistines. Then Saul will give up searching for me anywhere in Israel, and I will slip out of his hand (1 Samuel 27:1).

In the past, David talked to Gad or to one of his other counselors. Or better yet, he "inquired of the LORD" (1 Samuel 23:2,4). But on this occasion, David didn't ask the Lord or anyone else. He looked at his circumstances, took counsel of his fears, and fled to Philistia. Under the circumstances, he believed that was the best thing for him to do.

The phrase translated "The best thing I can do is to escape" is put in a way that suggests great haste: "I shall immediately escape. I will do it now!"

Decisions made when we're down in the dumps or emotionally distraught are exceedingly perilous. We're most vulnerable to bad choices when we're in that state of mind—choices we would never make if we were on top of things. When we're down, we inevitably stumble into bad judgment.

I wonder how many single people have decided in a moment of weariness that they can't handle the thought of perpetual loneliness, so they settle for a mate who makes life even more miserable for them? I wonder how many men have walked away from good jobs in a fit of momentary frustration and rage and now find themselves hopelessly out of work or working in situations far less desirable? I wonder how many have given up on their marriages when they are at low ebb and have lived to regret that decision? I wonder how many men have walked away from fruitful ministries because of weariness and discouragement?

Ignatius of Loyola, a sixteenth-century Basque Christian, wrote a book titled *The Spiritual Exercises*. He pointed out that there are two conditions in the Christian life. One is consolation, "When the soul is aroused to a love for its Creator and Lord. When faith, hope, and charity, and interior joy inspire the soul to peace and quiet in our Lord." The other is desolation, "When there is darkness of soul, turmoil of mind, a strong inclination to earthly things, restlessness resulting from disturbances, and temptations leading to loss of faith. We find ourselves apathetic, tepid, sad, and separated, as it were, from our Lord.

"In time of desolation," he continued, "one should never make a change, but stand firm and constant in the resolution and decision which guided him the day before the desolation, or to the decision which he observed in the preceding consolation. For just as the good spirit guides and consoles us in consolation, so in desolation the evil spirit guides and counsels. Following the counsels of this latter spirit, one can never find the correct way to a right decision."

He continued: "Although in desolation we should not change our earlier resolutions, it will be very advantageous to intensify our activity against desolation. This can be done by insisting more on prayer, meditation, examination, and confession."

So we should wait and pray. David eventually learned to wait for God (Psalm 5:3; 27:14; 33:20; 37:7,34; 38:15). He should have waited on this occasion, but he had made up his mind. Given his circumstances, Philistia looked better than the shadow of God's invisible wings.

*David and the six hundred men with him left and
went over to Achish son of Maoch king of Gath.
David and his men settled in Gath with Achish.
Each man had his family with him, and David
had his two wives: Ahinoam of Jezreel and
Abigail of Carmel, the widow of Nabal. When
Saul was told that David had fled to Gath, he no
longer searched for him (1 Samuel 27:2-4).*

■ DAVID'S RESTLESSNESS

David was safe in Gath, though increasingly
uneasy. His movements were restricted. He had
to give up his autonomy and independence. He
felt the need to get away from the royal city, so
he asked Achish for another place to live. It was a
modest request:

*David said to Achish, "If I have found favor
in your eyes, let a place be assigned to me in one
of the country towns, that I may live there.
Why should your servant live in the royal city
with you?" So on that day Achish gave him
Ziklag, and it has belonged to the kings of
Judah ever since. David lived in Philistine
territory a year and four months (27:5-7).*

At last David and his band could settle down.
For months their lives had been full of alarm and
flight. Now they had a little corner of peace. Their
children could play in safety. Old men and women
could sit in the sun and chat. Men could work the

fields instead of sustaining themselves by raiding and looting.

David and his people lived in Ziklag unmolested for a time, and everything seemed to be going well outwardly. But this was a barren time in David's walk with God. He wrote no poetry and sang no songs in Ziklag. Israel's sweet singer was mute. David drifted steadily away from the Lord.

But David's drifting did not result in personal failure alone—he also placed his friends in spiritual jeopardy. Philistia lay outside the inheritance of the Lord, the abiding place of the Most High. It was full of idols (2 Samuel 5:21).

As David drifted away from God, he became increasingly restless—a state of mind that always gets us in deep trouble.

■ DAVID'S TERRORIZING RAIDS

Now David and his men went up and raided the Geshurites, the Girzites and the Amalekites. (From ancient times these peoples had lived in the land extending to Shur and Egypt.) Whenever David attacked an area, he did not leave a man or woman alive, but took sheep and cattle, donkeys and camels, and clothes. Then he returned to Achish. When Achish asked, "Where did you go raiding today?" David would say, "Against the Negev of Judah" or "Against the Negev of Jerahmeel" or "Against the Negev of the Kenites." He did not leave a man or woman alive to be brought to

Gath, for he thought, "They might inform on
us and say, 'This is what David did.' "
And such was his practice as long as he
lived in Philistine territory. Achish trusted
David and said to himself, "He has become so
odious to his people, the Israelites, that he will
be my servant forever" (1 *Sam.* 27:8-12).

David plundered and looted village after village
and distributed the spoils to his kinsmen in Judah
(1 Sam. 30:26). But there is a jarring note in the
narrative. David adopted a policy of extermination—killing men, women, and children, lest they
inform on him. The verbs *attacked, leave,* and *took*
are what grammarians call "frequentative verbs"
describing habitual action. Extermination was his
"policy," as the Hebrew text described it, "as long
as he lived in Philistine territory." David ran in the
fast lane for one year and four months.

■ DAVID'S DECEIT

As the king's liege, David was obliged to report
on his battles and share some of the booty from
his victories. Achish would ask him, "Where did
you go raiding today?" David would lie, I've been
raiding Israelites and their allies—the Jerahmeelites
and the Kenites."

David embarked on a course that demanded
perpetual deceit. He had to keep lying to Achish, a
deception utterly unworthy of his character. Achish
accepted David's reports as evidence of his hatred

for Israel, thinking David had alienated himself from his countrymen and was now wholly in his service. "He has become so odious to his people," he said, "that he will be my servant forever" (27:12).

That's an interesting phrase: "He will be my servant forever." David, God's free spirit, had sold himself to serve a pagan king. "From wrong to wrong the exasperated spirit proceeds," T. S. Eliot said, "unless restored by that refining fire."

■ DAVID'S MOMENT OF TRUTH

The Philistines gathered their forces at Aphek to go to war against Israel. They were aware of the disintegration of Saul's kingdom and had noted with great satisfaction the growing number of mighty men who were abandoning Saul and identifying themselves with David and, presumably, with the Philistine army.

The Philistines decided to strike a final blow. So they gathered all their forces—along with David and his mercenaries—with the intent of assaulting Israel across the plain of Esdraelon. David was obliged to follow his king into battle, though he did so with a sinking heart. He knew he must go into battle against his own countrymen, against Saul his king, and against Jonathan his beloved friend.

It may be that at this point David's heart began to turn to God, asking Him to extricate him from the mess he had contrived for himself. If so, the Lord heard him.

F. B. Meyer has written, "If by your mistakes and sins you have reduced yourself into a false position like this, do not despair; hope still in God. Confess and put away your sin, and humble yourself before Him and He will arise to deliver you. You may have destroyed yourself, but in Him will be your help."

A door of hope was opened. On the eve of the encounter, God intervened. The Philistines themselves insisted that David and his men have no part in the battle, so they turned with relief to their homes in Ziklag.

> *David and his men reached Ziklag on the third day. Now the Amalekites had raided the Negev and Ziklag. They had attacked Ziklag and burned it, and had taken captive the women and all who were in it, both young and old. They killed none of them, but carried them off as they went on their way. When David and his men came to Ziklag, they found it destroyed by fire and their wives and sons and daughters taken captive. So David and his men wept aloud until they had no strength left to weep (30:1-4).*

David and his men had been on the road for days and were exhausted, eagerly anticipating seeing their wives and children. As they neared Ziklag, they saw a plume of smoke on the horizon and ran the last few miles to Ziklag to find the city torched and their women and little ones kidnapped. Instead of happy reunion, there was eerie silence and desolation. There were only a few elderly men and women left to tell the story. David and his men wept until they could weep no more.

David's troops turned and glared at him in angry silence. There was talk of lynching him. David was personally responsible for their loss, and he knew it. He should have left a few men to guard the city. He should have known. He had let his men down. You can imagine his terrible sense of isolation.

And then there was his own personal loss. There was no hope, no human prospect of redeeming the situation. He could never catch the Amalekites. They were mounted on camels and long gone. When we have hope, we can endure. When we are robbed of hope, life loses all its meaning.

David sensed the righteous judgment of God. His conscience awoke and began to speak. David had been leading a double life—betraying Achish and raiding Philistine allies. He had massacred whole villages and then had lied. Now his village and family were gone. This was one of the darkest moments in David's life.

■ DAVID'S REPENTANCE

David wept in misery and despair. He wept until he could weep no more. A perfectly natural reaction. But the natural is fatal. "By sorrow of the heart the spirit is broken" the proverb says (Proverbs 15:13 NKJV).

David was greatly distressed because the men were

talking of stoning him, each one was bitter in spirit because of his sons and daughters. But David found strength in the LORD his God (1 Samuel 30:6).

"David was greatly distressed," but he "found strength in the Lord his God." The Hebrew text reads, "He strengthened himself in the Lord." That is one of the greatest lines in the Bible.

Once again, David referred to God as his God! No doubt David's men had heard him say repeatedly, "The Lord is my shepherd, my rock, my salvation." Although David had seriously compromised God's name by his failure of faith and his torturous and treacherous policies, the Lord was still his God. And in the present crisis he could flee to the shelter of His wings.

God never refuses His help, even when we have brought ruin upon ourselves. Regardless of what we have done, we must run to Him and take His strong hand. The man who can come to God with the weight of failure on his mind and say to Him, "You are my refuge," is the man who understands the gracious heart of God.

David "strengthened himself in the Lord." He must have gone back to God's promises of forgiveness and restoration, which so often cheered him at other dark periods of his life. He must have recalled the poems he wrote on other dark days like this that reflected God's faithfulness. He must have remembered that he had been in worse situations than this and that God had greatly helped him in those times. Although his faith had been sorely tested, it had not been disappointed. In this way he encouraged himself.

All around David was frustration and fear. But God was at hand, "An ever-present help in trouble" (Psalm 46:1). David took strength from God and became a center of peace. Remember Paul's words, "Be men of courage; be strong" (1 Corinthians 16:13).

■ DAVID'S RECOVERY

David, in the end, recovered everything the Amalekites had stolen, including his family (1 Samuel 30:18-19). But not all our failures will turn out that way. There are no guarantees in this life that we will get back the family, the business, the reputation we have lost through our foolishness.

We may reach the end of our years a long way from our goals. We may be known more for our failures than for our successes. We may not be powerful or prosperous. But if we accept the disappointment and let it draw us close to God, we will find in time that our failure has given us a deeper understanding of His love and grace. That is by far the better thing.

It requires enormous faith to believe that our failures are for the greater good. But it is true. We learn far more from disappointment than we do from success. We come to know God and His ways. The man who has never failed has never made that discovery.

DAVID:
Overcoming Moral Failure

I KEEP SEEING MY FRIENDS FALL. I wonder why they do it. What causes a man to trash his marriage and all he's worked for, for a transient affair? Take David, for example—Israel's greatest king, the "man after God's own heart." He fell for Uriah's pretty, young wife, Bathsheba.

It happened "in the spring, at the time when kings go off to war" (2 Samuel 11:1). That spring, however, in fatal lethargy, David's energies became focused elsewhere. "One evening David got up from his bed and walked around on the roof of the palace" (v. 2).

From there, he had a commanding view of Jerusalem and could look down into neighboring courtyards. As he surveyed his city, his eyes fell upon a young woman taking a bath. The text says she was very beautiful (v. 2).

If the woman seems immodest, you must remember there was no indoor plumbing in those days. Baths were normally taken outdoors in enclosed courtyards.

David was entranced! He sent someone "to find out about her" (v. 3), whereupon, one of his friends tried to discourage him. "Isn't this Bathsheba, the daughter of Eliam and the wife of Uriah the Hittite?" (v. 3) he asked. She was a married woman—married in fact to Uriah, one of David's mighty men, a member of David's exclusive bodyguard (23:39).

David, however, would not be denied. He "sent messengers to get her." One wrong thing led to another and "he slept with her . . . Then she went back home." Later, we're told, She "sent word to David, saying, 'I am pregnant' " (11:4-5).

David knew he was in big trouble! Bathsheba's husband was engaged in the siege of the Ammonite city of Rabbah and would be away for several months. Anyone could count to nine. In other lands kings were the law, but not in Israel. No one was above God's Word. Adultery was serious sin.

But David, always a man of action, devised a plan to avert the consequences of his affair. He sent word to Joab to release Uriah from his command and send him to Jerusalem, ostensibly to report on the war, but in reality to bring him home to Bathsheba. When the old warrior arrived, David listened to his briefing and then dismissed Uriah to his home: "Go down to your house and wash your feet" (v.8), he said with a twinkle in his eye.

But Uriah "slept at the entrance to the palace wall his master's servants and did not go down to his house" (v. 9). When David asked why he did not go home, Uriah explained, "The ark and Israel and Judah are staying in tents, and my master Joab and my lord's men are camping in the open fields. How could I go to my house to eat and drink and lie with my wife? As surely as you live, I will not do such a thing!" (v. 11).

David replied, " 'Stay here one more day, and tomorrow I will send you back.' So Uriah remained in Jerusalem that day and the next. At David's invitation, he ate and drank with him, and David made him drunk. But in the evening Uriah went out to sleep on his mat among his master's servants; he did not go home" (11:12-13).

Uriah would not go home while those under his command were separated from their wives and families. Despite David's repeated efforts to persuade Uriah, the stern, old Hittite refused. Even getting him drunk failed. Each evening Uriah rolled out his sleeping bag on the floor of the palace guardroom and slept with the rest of the troops.

Time was running out. In desperation David put a contract on his life, ordering General Joab to "put Uriah in the front line where the fighting is fiercest. Then withdraw from him so he will be struck down and die" (v. 15).

Joab, who was no fool, refused to follow David's directive. The plan was so obviously treacherous that he altered it: "While Joab had the city under siege, he put Uriah at a place where he knew the strongest defenders were. When the men of the city came out and fought against Joab, some of the men in David's army fell; moreover, Uriah the Hittite died" (vv. 16-17).

Joab then sent a runner to David with a report on the battle. He knew David would be critical of his tactics and the resultant loss of life, but he hastened to report that Uriah had been killed (vv. 18-22).

David didn't want Joab to be upset so he said, "The sword devours one as well as another" (v. 25).

When Bathsheba heard that her husband was dead, she mourned for him. When her brief period of mourning was over, David "had her brought to his house, and she became his wife and bore him a son" (v. 27).

David moved with inappropriate haste, but marriage put a legal and final end to the sordid affair— or so David thought. But God knew, and "the thing David had done displeased the Lord" (v. 27).

A year passed, during which time David deteriorated physically and emotionally. He later described his feelings:

> *When I kept silent, my bones wasted away through my groaning all day long. For day and night Your hand was heavy upon me; my strength was sapped as in the heat of summer (Psalms 32:3-4).*

His gnawing conscience kept him restless and melancholy. Every waking moment was filled with misery. At night he tossed and turned. Anxiety sapped his energy. His depression deepened with every passing day.

Eventually, David had to face the facts. To be more precise, he had to face the prophet Nathan, who knew the truth. Nathan trapped the shepherd-king with a story about a rich man who had vast flocks of sheep but who seized another man's pet lamb to serve to a traveling stranger (2 Samuel 12:4).

David was enraged, and at first he overreacted

out of moral outrage: "As surely as the Lord lives, the man who did this deserves to die!" But sheepnapping was not a capital offense in Israel. According to Exodus 22:1, a thief was only required to make fourfold restitution to the victim. David then said, "He must pay for that lamb four times over, because he did such a thing and had no pity" (v. 5).

Nathan drove his verdict home.

> "You are the man! This is what the LORD, the God of Israel, says: 'I anointed you king over Israel, and I delivered you from the hand of Saul. I gave your master's house to you, and your master's wives into your arms. I gave you the house of Israel and Judah. And if all this had been too little, I would have given you even more. Why did you despise the word of the Lord by doing what is evil in his eyes?" (2 Samuel 12:7-9).

When he was brought face to face with his corruption, David's defenses crumbled. Burying his face in his hands, he cried, "I have sinned against the Lord." And Nathan replied, "The Lord has taken away your sin. You are not going to die" (v.13).

To David's credit, he did not try to justify himself. He acknowledged his sin, and God immediately canceled the handwriting that was against him. David could lift up his head. As he later wrote:

> I acknowledged my sin to you and did not cover up my iniquity. I said, "I will confess my transgressions to the Lord"—and you forgave the guilt of my sin (Psalms 32:5).

As the apostle John promised, "If we confess [acknowledge] our sins, He is faithful and just and will forgive us our sins and purify us from all unrighteousness" (1 John 1:9). Happiness is knowing that our sins have been forgiven.

Blessed [happy] is he whose transgressions are forgiven, whose sins are covered. Blessed [happy] is the man whose sin the LORD *does not count against him and in whose spirit is no deceit* (Psalms 32:1-2).

David bore terrible consequences for his sin. Nathan predicted that he would suffer:

The sword will never depart from your house, because you despised [God] and took the wife of Uriah the Hittite to be your own. This is what the Lord says: "Out of your own household I am going to bring calamity upon you. Before your very eyes I will take your wives and give them to one who is close to you, and he will lie with your wives in broad daylight. You did it in secret, but I will do this thing in broad daylight before all Israel. . . . Because by doing this you have made the enemies of the Lord show utter contempt, the son born to you will die" (2 Samuel 12:10-12, 14).

David paid dearly for his few moments of pleasure. His family life and political career came apart at the seams from that time on. All that Nathan had predicted came true.

God cannot be mocked. A man reaps what he sows (Galatians 6:7).

But David could rise from his fall to walk with God. "No amount of falls will really undo us," wrote C. S. Lewis, "if we keep picking ourselves up each time. We shall of course be very muddy and tattered children by the time we reach home The only fatal thing is to lose one's temper and give up."

■ THE LAW OF INEVITABLE SEQUENCE

Reading David's story and watching my friends fall has led me to one conclusion: Moral collapse is rarely a blowout; it's more like a slow leak—the result of a thousand small indulgences. Very few people plan an adulterous affair; they transition into it.

It begins with attraction. It's not lust as much as infatuation that brings us down. We're drawn to someone sensitive and understanding, someone who listens and seems to care. We're seduced by that attraction and led on by subtle degrees.

Attraction becomes fantasy: We imagine ourselves with that person and the feeling is good. Fictionalized affairs always seem so right. That's their fundamental deception.

The fantasies soften us, and our convictions erode. We're then in a frame of mind to listen to our longings, and having listened we have no will to resist. We cannot escape the realization of our predominant thoughts.

Then there are the meetings and the sharing of

inner conflict, marital disappointment, and other deep hurts. And with that sharing, the relationship begins to shift. We're suddenly two lonely people in need of one another's love.

Then comes the inevitable yielding, and with that yielding the need to justify the affair. We can't live with the dissonance. We have to rationalize our behavior by blaming someone or something else—the pressures of our business or the limitations of our spouses. Others' wrongdoing becomes our reason. Everything must be made to look good.

But our hearts know. There are moments when our wills soften and we long to set things right. If we do not then listen to our hearts, there comes a metallic hardening, and then corruption. Our wrongdoing mutates, altering its form and quality, evolving into dark narcissism and horrifying cruelty. We don't care who gets hurt as long as we get what we want.

And finally there is inevitable disclosure. First we deny: "There's no one else!" Then we dissemble: "It's only platonic." And finally our deception is shouted from the housetops. There's no place to hide from the light.

When our seams have been opened and our evil deeds have been exposed, God reminds us of His cross, His forgiveness, and His incomparable grace. Then He begins to make us new.

But there's only one way to know that forgiveness: acknowledgment of the awfulness of one's sin and that old-fashioned word, *repentance*. We must hate what we've done and turn from it in disgust.

That's what Paul calls "godly sorrow [that] brings repentance that leads to salvation and leaves no regret" (2 Corinthians 7:10). Ungodly sorrow is the sorrow of being found out, or of suffering the consequences of being found out. The result is intensified guilt, anxiety, and hopelessness. Godly sorrow, on the other hand, is sorrow over sin itself and the harm that it has done to others. Godly sorrow asserts itself to set things right.

Here's the way Paul put it:

> *"See what this godly sorrow has produced in you: what earnestness [to obey], what eagerness to clear yourselves [of wrongdoing], what indignation [against evil], what alarm [that we might fall into sin again], what longing [for purity], what concern [for all those damaged by our sin], what readiness to see justice [righteousness] done"* (2 Corinthians 7:11).

As David himself learned, "The sacrifices of God are a broken spirit; a broken and contrite heart, O God, you will not despise" (Psalm 51:17). God discerns the possibilities even in our defilement, forgives our sins, counteracts our mistakes, and gives us opportunities to be better than we've ever been before.

Therefore, rather than mourn our humiliation, we must move on. Sin may have consequences with which we must live for the rest of our natural lives, but repentance of sin can only work for ultimate good. God takes the worst that we can do and makes it part of the good He has promised. He's the God of fools and failures and the God of another chance.

Four

MARY & MARTHA

Balancing Life's Priorities

lice Mathews uses the experiences of her life and heart to bring fresh perspective to the Word of God. She has been a missionary, a pastor's wife, a mother, and a grandmother. Now with an earned doctorate, she's a chaired Professor at Gordon-Conwell Seminary.

It takes a busy woman to understand the heart of Martha, a busy, overworked woman in the New Testament. It also takes a reflective woman who loves to learn at the feet of her Lord to understand the heart of Martha's sister, Mary.

I believe Alice is just such a woman. And she shares her insights about Mary and Martha in the following pages.

—*Martin R. De Haan II*

MARY & MARTHA:
How To Live Successfully In Two Worlds

WHEN I ENTERED FIFTH GRADE, I began studying what was then called "domestic science." By the time I reached high school, the name had changed to "home economics." I understand college course catalogs now label it "human ecology." By any name it was the same: a semester of cooking, a semester of sewing, a semester of cooking, a semester of sewing. You may have found yourself in a similar track.

I'm not sure which I hated most—the cooking or the sewing. At age ten I could not separate eggs neatly or make decent flat-felled seams. I remember mostly that I dreaded the hours spent in the domestic science rooms.

We learned to sew using treadle machines. No electric wizards then. When I stopped recently at a fabric store for a pattern, I glanced at the array of modern sewing machines on display— wonderful electronic computerized miracle workers! While I stood there admiring technology in the service of seamstresses, I also noticed one thing that has hardly changed since my first introduction to domestic science fifty years ago. On the front of the sewing machine just above the needle is a dial that adjusts the tension on the thread as the machine sews.

For a strong, firm seam a thread from the spool above and another thread from the bobbin below must interlock smoothly and tightly in the fabric. An experienced seamstress checks the thread tension and makes minute adjustments in setting that dial because she understands how important it is that the tension be regulated properly.

At times as I sew, I accidentally bump that dial. I hear the click-click that tells me I've messed up the delicate balance of upper and lower threads. I know that no seams will be strong and usable until I get the tension adjusted again. Everything else has to stop until I'm satisfied that the threads are interlocking properly.

As I read through Luke 10:38-42 recently, I thought about the tension dial on my sewing machine. Luke wrote about a dinner party held in a home in Bethany:

> *As Jesus and his disciples were on their way, he came to a village where a woman named Martha opened her home to him. She had a sister called Mary, who sat at the Lord's feet listening to what he said. But Martha was distracted by all the preparations that had to be made. She came to him and asked, "Lord, don't you care that my sister has left me to do the work by myself? Tell her to help me!"*
>
> *"Martha, Martha," the Lord answered, "you are worried and upset about many things, but only one thing is needed. Mary has chosen what is better, and it will not be taken away from her."*

Here's the scene: A hot day at the end of the rainy season as summer was beginning. A white-washed village on a hillside just two miles east of Jerusalem. The home of Martha, who was possibly a well-to-do widow who had taken in her younger sister Mary and younger brother Lazarus.

She welcomes Jesus and His followers to her home in Bethany. She hurries to arrange a comfort-able seat for Jesus and then to bring a cool drink to each of her guests. She nods to Mary, who fills the basin near the door with water, then takes a towel and begins to wash each guest's feet. Jesus' follow-ers seat themselves around the large room, chatting quietly about events of recent days. Villagers begin to crowd the doorway, anxious to come in and listen to the great Rabbi, Jesus.

This is not His first visit to Bethany. The townsfolk have heard some of His surprising stories before. Perhaps He will tell them more. A few edge in and sit down outside the ring of disciples. It's pos-sible that both Martha and Mary take their places at Jesus' feet to learn from Him. (Luke 10:39 in the NKJV says that Mary *also* sat at Jesus' feet.")

I don't know how long Martha sat there listen-ing to the Lord Jesus. But I have a feeling that if she was anything like me, she sat there that day with a divided mind. After all, here were thirteen men who would be hungry and needed to be fed. What was on hand to feed them? What would it take to get everything ready? Would she need to slip out and run to a few shops for grain or fruit?

I identify with Martha. I know exactly what she was doing as she sat there. First, she made a mental inventory of everything in the pantry. After that, she planned the menu, making sure she didn't overlook anything. Then she made a list in her head of all the tasks that would have to be done. When she had thought everything through, she glanced around the room surreptitiously to see the best route through the crowd to get from where she was sitting into the kitchen. When she had plotted her exit, she could sit there no longer. She had to get busy! After all, she was the hostess. It was her responsibility to meet the needs of her guests. No one would think less of Lazarus or Mary if the meal were not adequate. The blame would land squarely on her. No time to sit and listen to Jesus now—perhaps after all the work was done.

Once in the kitchen, she felt that flush of excitement that comes to many of us when we are about to do something special for someone we really care about. We want everything to be perfect—well, at least as nearly perfect as possible. Our love energizes us. We are exhilarated by the opportunity to show our love for someone special.

Can you see Martha, now in the familiar territory of her kitchen, turning into a whirlwind of activity? First, start the beans and lentils cooking with onions and garlic. Then dress the lamb for roasting. Grind the grain and mix the bread for baking. Then prepare the figs and pomegranates. Get water to mix with the wine. Set the table. Stir the beans and lentils. Turn the lamb on the spit. Start baking the bread.

Glancing out the window at the position of the sun in the sky, Martha suddenly realized it would soon be mealtime and she was far from finished. She may have felt what I feel when I've been carried along on the crest of my enthusiasm, only to realize I'm running out of time and I can't finish everything I planned to do. When that happens, I get angry—angry with myself and angry with anyone else who might have made a difference in accomplishing my plans.

I suspect that is what happened to Martha. Suddenly the plans and the work that had started out as pure joy turned sour. Luke tells us in verse 40 that she was distracted by all the preparations she was making. The harder she worked, the more worked up she became.

It was Mary's fault. If Mary had been there to help her, it would have been different.

We all know that feeling, don't we? It's bad enough having everything to do. It's even worse when someone we think should be helping us pull the load lets us down. Our irritation about the unfairness of it all builds to the bursting point.

That's what happened to Martha. In verse 40, she finally explodes:

Lord, don't you care that my sister has left me to do the work by myself? Tell her to help me!

Interesting, isn't it, that Martha spoke her irritation to Jesus, not to Mary. Perhaps she had already tried unsuccessfully to catch Mary's eye and signal her to get up and help. Or she may have nudged Mary, who shook off her nudge and went on listening to Jesus.

We all have ways we use to get a message across. We clear our throat. We drum our fingers on the tabletop. We make attention-getting motions. It irritates us even more when the other person ignores us!

Whatever had already happened, Martha spoke directly to Jesus, accusing Him of not caring about her. She was sure that, if He really cared, He would tell Mary to get up and help her.

I'm intrigued by the way Martha linked Jesus' care for her to His willingness to tell Mary to get busy. Martha thought she knew just how Jesus should demonstrate His care—by lightening her load.

That is exactly what we see Him doing, though not in the way she expected. In His response we learn much about our discipleship as Christian women:

Martha, Martha, . . . you are worried and upset about many things, but only one thing is needed. Mary has chosen what is better, and it will not be taken away from her (Luke 10:41-42).

The problem did not lie in the work Martha was doing. It was her attitude of fretting and worrying that created the bad situation. Jesus knew that Martha put too much stress on things that didn't matter. Martha's problem was one of balance, of holding life in the proper tension. Take a closer look at what Jesus said and did not say to this overburdened woman.

First, Jesus did not rebuke her for making preparations for Him and His disciples. If she as the hostess in the home had decided to skip any food preparation, her guests would have gone hungry. What was going on in that Bethany kitchen was important.

Do you recall what Jesus had said to Satan when tempted in the wilderness at the outset of His public ministry? In Matthew 4:4 we read, "Man does not live on bread alone." Jesus did not say, "People don't live on bread." We do live on bread. We have bodies that must be fed. Jesus knew that and fed people—as many as 5,000 at one time.

But Jesus also knew that people are more than bodies. We do not live on bread alone. To feed our spirits is at least as important as feeding our bodies. Martha's problem was not that she was preparing food for her guests to eat. That was necessary, and in her role as hostess, it was her place to see that it was done. But she gave it too much importance. Instead of settling for a simple supper, she tried to impress with an elaborate meal. Jesus in essence told her that one dish would have been enough.

We all have responsibilities we carry out every day of our lives. We go to the office. We cook. We grade papers. We clean the house. We do the laundry. We do these things, and we want to do them well. Dorothy Sayers reminds us that no crooked table legs came out of the carpenter shop in Nazareth. God is not honored by shoddy work or the neglect of our necessary duties in life.

But we must be sure that the necessary doesn't get out of proportion and distort our lives. We can easily confuse means and ends. Without thinking, we can turn what is a means of living for God into an end in itself. When we take something that is not too important and make it primary in our lives, what is otherwise harmless can become a stumbling block for us.

One of the things Jesus saw that afternoon 2,000 years ago was that Martha was looking down on what Mary had chosen to do. Martha imposed her value system—possibly a sparkling house and certainly a sumptuous meal—on Mary. If bustling around was "necessary" for Martha, it must also be necessary for Mary.

Note that Jesus did not tell Martha to do what Mary was doing. At the same time, He pointed out that Mary had chosen the good part. In saying this, Jesus made a little play on words that does not come through in English translations. In essence He said, "Martha, you are preparing many dishes for us to eat, but Mary has prepared the one dish you can't fix in your kitchen." While food was necessary, something much simpler would have been better, allowing Martha to continue sitting with Mary and learning from Christ.

Do you think Jesus was being a bit hard on Martha? After all, she was doing all this work to please Him! Yet do you think He was pleased with her request that He tell Mary to get up and help her? Do you think Mary was pleased to be humiliated in that way? Do you think the disciples and neighbors were pleased to have the Teacher interrupted in that way? And what about Martha herself? Do you think she was pleased with herself? We know when we have spoiled things for ourselves and others around us. And spoil things Martha did!

As you picture this scene in your mind, what image of Martha comes into your head? Elisabeth Moltmann-Wendel remarked that whenever she thinks of Martha, she remembers a picture from a children's Bible. In it Mary is sitting at Jesus' feet listening and Martha is in the background, leaning against the kitchen door with an evil, mistrustful look on her face.

When we think about these two sisters, we tend to imagine Mary with an aura of holiness around her, and we associate Martha with olive oil and fish.

When someone says, "She's a Martha-type," we know just what that means. Someone who is practical, competent, down-to-earth. Marthas are certainly useful and necessary. The church would be in a tough spot if we were all Marys. But when it comes to painting a model or an ideal, it's Mary all the way. That puts us in a bind of sorts, if we think about it. Martha's work is necessary—in the church and in the home. But Mary gets the halo.

Martha, called the patron saint of housewives and cooks, comes in for quite a bit of bashing. Martin Luther wrote, "Martha, your work must be punished and counted as naught . . . . I will have no work but the work of Mary."

Stiff words! So I feel a bit sheepish about being a Martha. But Martin Luther was wrong. Martha's work must not be punished and counted as naught. Martha's attitude needed correcting. Martha's perspective needed changing. But Martha's work is good and necessary. The reality is that as followers of Jesus Christ we need to cultivate both the Martha and the Mary in each of us.

Earlier in Luke 10 we find the story of a lawyer who tried to trap Jesus by asking Him what he had to do to inherit eternal life. Jesus turned the question back on the lawyer by asking him simply, "What is written in the Law? How do you read it?" The lawyer responded with two great statements taken from Deuteronomy 6:5 and Leviticus 19:18— we are to love the Lord our God with all our heart, with all our soul, with all our strength, and with all our mind, and our neighbor as ourselves.

The lawyer got the answer absolutely right. Jesus agreed, saying, "You have answered correctly. Do this and you will live."

The lawyer could have left it at that, but he didn't. He pressed Jesus with another question: "And who is my neighbor?" To answer that, Jesus told one of those wonderful stories that take us by surprise.

The story was about a man traveling from

Jerusalem down to Jericho on a dusty mountain road. Some thieves attacked him, stripped him naked, beat him, and left him half dead. First, a priest came by. He might have just finished his week of service rotation in Jerusalem and was on his way home for another year. He saw this poor man but went out of his way to avoid any contact with him. Then a Levite came along. Levites in first-century Israel were lower-order priests who sang at the time of the sacrifice and who served as doorkeepers and servants to the higher-order priests. The Levite, like the priest, glanced at the injured man and passed by on the other side of the road.

The third person who came along was a Samaritan, despised by the Jews. You have to know how much Jews detested Samaritans to have any idea how shocking this story was that Jesus would say a Samaritan came along. This despised foreigner saw the man, and instead of doing what the religious Jews had done, he stopped and dressed and bandaged the poor man's wounds, put the man on his donkey, and took him to an inn where he cared for him. He even paid the innkeeper to continue caring for the man while he went on his way.

What was the punch line? When Jesus finished the story, He asked the lawyer who he thought was a neighbor to the injured man. Of course, the lawyer had to say, "The one who had mercy on him" (v. 37). And Jesus answered, "Go and do likewise."

Wasn't that just what Martha had done? Hadn't she inconvenienced herself to treat Jesus and His disciples kindly? Wasn't she meeting someone else's need? Absolutely! Wasn't she being a "good Samaritan" while Mary ignored the physical needs of their guests as the two religious Jews had ignored the man who was beaten and robbed?

Take a second look at the answer for which Jesus commended that first-century lawyer: We are to love the Lord our God with all our heart, with all our soul, with all our strength, and with all our mind, and our neighbor as ourselves.

Note the order of the two loves: God first, then neighbor. Not the other way around. It is not a question of contrasting the activist life to the contemplative life. It's a matter of priorities. We put listening to and learning the Word of God before service. That equips and inspires us for our service for God and to others.

What Jesus wanted that day was not Martha's lentils and lamb, but Martha herself. The one dish she could not prepare in her kitchen was her relationship to God. She could prepare that dish only by remaining at Jesus' feet and letting Him provide the food for her soul.

Martha wanted Jesus to lighten her load that day. He did exactly that, but not the way she thought it should be done. He knew that our relationship with God does not develop in the midst of fretting busyness. The one thing needful is to hear God speak to us. Mary chose to put time into that primary relationship and not to be distracted by trivia.

"Martha must be a Mary," wrote one commentator, "and the true Mary must also be a Martha; both are sisters." That brings me back to my sewing machine tension dial. If the tension on the top thread is too loose, the underside of the fabric will be snarled with excess thread. The seam has no strength. It pulls apart hopelessly the moment pressure is applied to it. The only thing a seamstress can do is pull out all the threads, adjust the tension, and start over.

We also have no usable seam if the threads are not feeding from both the top spool and the bobbin underneath. We could try to sew all day with only the top spool on the machine and nothing in the bobbin holder. We would not have a single seam. The Martha thread and the Mary thread must both be properly feeding and interlocking if we are to have any seam at all. The balance between the two has to be finely adjusted if the resulting seam is to be strong and usable.

We live in this world. This means we concern ourselves with food and clothes and homes and family and jobs and studies. But we also live in the world of the spirit. We concern ourselves with our relationship to God. That was Martha's real problem. She was sewing with no thread in the bobbin.

To get our service right, we get our priorities right. We let Jesus minister to us before we go out to minister for Him. That is God's order: we first love the Lord our God with all our heart, soul, strength, and mind, and then we are prepared to go out and love our neighbor as ourselves. When we turn that upside down, we may end up feeling overworked and unappreciated. When we keep our priorities in line with God's priorities, we will find that God enables us to do what needs to be done with joy and satisfaction.

MARTHA & MARY:
How To Nourish Hope In Times Of Loss

WHEN MY HUSBAND finished his studies at Denver Seminary in 1956, we moved to his first pastorate in a small town in central Wyoming. As we got acquainted with the leaders of the church, we came to appreciate one older couple in particular. Gene, a retired carpenter, arrived at the church every morning to help build an addition to the church education wing. Mae stopped by almost as often. We admired the tireless commitment to Jesus Christ and to His church they both lived in front of us daily. About six months after we arrived, a phone call brought the news that their only son Don had just been crushed to death in a local open-pit mine accident. We hurried across town to be with Gene and Mae, who we knew would be struggling with shock and disbelief. It would be an excruciating time for them as they moved through their grief. But we were sure they would make it. They had all the

Christian resources to support them during this crisis. Other friends came in, and we were confident that an entire community would surround them, their daughter-in-law, and two grandsons with love and concern.

A few days after the funeral Gene returned to his volunteer work on the church building. But on Sundays he came to church alone. When we dropped by their house, we sensed that Gene was finding strength to cope with his grief, but it was different for Mae.

When we asked about this, we learned that from the time word of the accident came, Mae turned her back on God. How could she believe in a God who would deny them their only child and deny their grandsons a father? God could not possibly be loving and kind and, at the same time, deal them such a blow. Whenever we visited her, we listened to her case against God. It was clear that the facts of her faith and the facts of her life didn't mesh. The faith that we thought would sustain her seemed to get in her way.

Mae's situation reminded me of two other women—women who sent for Jesus when their brother was seriously ill. But Jesus didn't arrive in time to help them. When He finally showed up, both women said to Him, "Lord, if you had been here, our brother wouldn't have died!" These sisters had enough faith to believe that if Jesus had come He could have healed their brother. But it looked as if Jesus had let them down.

The story is found in John 11. The first six verses tell us this:

> *Now a man named Lazarus was sick. He was from Bethany, the village of Mary and her sister Martha. This Mary, whose brother Lazarus now lay sick, was the same one who poured perfume on the Lord and wiped his feet with her hair. So the sisters sent word to Jesus, "Lord, the one you love is sick." When he heard this, Jesus said, "This sickness will not end in death. No, it is for God's glory so that God's Son may be glorified through it." Jesus loved Martha and her sister and Lazarus. Yet when he heard that Lazarus was sick, he stayed where he was two more days.*

That's the setting. Lazarus was sick. His two sisters, Mary and Martha, turned at once to their friend Jesus, hoping He would come quickly and heal their brother before it was too late.

Knowing that Jesus loved this trio, we would expect Him to set out immediately for Bethany to do what He could to spare them anxiety and grief. Yet we see Jesus not responding in the way the two sisters hoped. Instead of leaving at once for Bethany, He stayed where He was two more days.

An important principle in life is that love permits pain. We don't want it that way. We want to believe that if God truly loves us He will not allow anything painful to invade our lives. But this is not so. God's love does not guarantee us a shelter from difficult experiences that are necessary for our spiritual growth. Love and delay are compatible.

If Jesus had rushed off to Bethany as soon as He received word of Lazarus' illness, Mary and Martha would not have been suspended between hope and fear—hope that the One who could help their brother would arrive in time yet fear that He might come too late. They would have been spared the anguish of watching Lazarus sink into death. They would have avoided the agony of those last moments before they closed Lazarus' eyes and prepared his body for burial. They would have forestalled the desolation of bereavement. But Jesus didn't come.

He knew that it was time for Mary, Martha, and His disciples to learn what they could not learn if He intervened too quickly. John 11 tells us how completely in control of the situation Jesus was. He knew just what He was doing. He knew that the spiritual growth of Martha and Mary and His band of disciples traveling with Him depended on the right timing. How do we know that? Read John 11:7-16.

Then he said to His disciples, "Let us go back to Judea." "But Rabbi," they said, "a short while ago the Jews tried to stone you, and yet you are going back there?" Jesus answered, "Are there not twelve hours of daylight? A man who walks by day will not stumble, for he sees by this world's light. It is when he walks by night that he stumbles, for he has no light." After he had said this, he went on to tell them, "Our friend Lazarus has fallen asleep;

but I am going there to wake him up." His disciples replied, "Lord, if he sleeps, he will get better." Jesus had been speaking of his death, but his disciples thought he meant natural sleep. So then he told them plainly, "Lazarus is dead, and for your sake I am glad I was not there, so that you may believe. But let us go to him." Then Thomas (called Didymus) said to the rest of the disciples, "Let us also go, that we may die with him."

Divine timing. Jesus knew that Mary and Martha would never know Him as the resurrection and the life if Lazarus had not died. David would not have known God as his rock and his fortress had he not been hunted by Saul in the mountains of En Gedi. The Israelites would not have known God as their deliverer had they not been slaves in Egypt. Our painful experiences can reveal God to us in new ways. Jesus knew precisely what He was doing.

On His arrival, Jesus found that Lazarus had been in the tomb for four days. Many Jews had come from Jerusalem to Bethany to comfort Martha and Mary in the loss of their brother. Sympathy for them was the first of all duties. Nothing else was more important than expressing sorrow with the bereaved.

In the hot climate of Israel the deceased had to be buried immediately after death. Women anointed the body with the finest spices and ointments, then wrapped it in a linen garment with the hands and feet swathed in bandage-like wrappings and the head enclosed in a towel. Everyone who could possibly come would join the procession from the house to the tomb. Curiously, women walked first because, according to the teachers of the day, it was a woman by her sin in the Garden of Eden who was responsible for death coming into the world.

At the tomb, friends made memorial speeches. Then the mourners formed two long lines between which the family members walked. As long as the dead body remained in the house, the family was forbidden to prepare food there, to eat meat or drink wine, or to study. When the body was carried out, all the furniture was turned upside-down and the mourners sat on the ground or on low stools. On returning from the tomb, they ate a meal of bread, hard-boiled eggs, and lentils, symbolizing life, which was always rolling toward death.

Deep mourning lasted seven days, during which no one could anoint himself, put on shoes, engage in study or business, or even wash. Thirty days of lighter mourning followed the week of heavy mourning.

In the middle of this period of deep mourning, Martha heard that Jesus was entering the village. Violating the conventions of the Middle East, she went out to meet Him while Mary stayed in the house. The remarkable conversation Martha and Jesus had is recorded in John 11:21-27.

"Lord," Martha said to Jesus, "if you had been here, my brother would not have died. But I know

that even now God will give you whatever you ask." Jesus said to her, "Your brother will rise again." Martha answered, "I know he will rise again in the resurrection at the last day." Jesus said to her, "I am the resurrection and the life. He who believes in me will live, even though he dies; and whoever lives and believes in me will never die. Do you believe this?" "Yes, Lord," she told him, "I believe that you are the Christ, the Son of God, who was to come into the world."

"Lord, if You had been here, my brother would not have died." In that statement Martha gave voice to her doubt that Jesus had unlimited power. Had He been there, this would not have happened. He had to be present to heal her brother. Yet her general confidence in Jesus shines through: "But I know that even now God will give You whatever You ask."

Jesus answered her by turning her mind to the promise of the resurrection: "Your brother will rise again." Martha seemed impatient as she shot back, "Yes, Lord, I know he will rise again in the resurrection at the last day."

She knew the truth. She had the doctrine down right. In fact, she had a stronger spiritual base than the Sadducees, who denied the resurrection. In her statement she bore witness to the strong teaching of her nation's faith. But she didn't find much comfort in the future tense. In that moment she needed something more immediate than an event as far off as "the resurrection at the

last day." The doctrine was not particularly consoling in her time of sorrow.

Jesus saw that and turned her idea of resurrection as a future event into a present reality: "I am the
resurrection and the life." What must Martha have
felt in that dramatic moment! "I am the resurrection and the life!" With those startling words Jesus
brought Martha's thoughts from a dim future hope
to a present fact. He gave her faith its true object,
himself. Confidence in Jesus Christ, the God-Man
who is the resurrection and the life, could replace
her vague hope in a future event.

How do we get that confidence? Jesus told us
how in verse 25: "He who believes in me will live,
even though he dies; and whoever lives and believes
in me will never die."

When we believe in Jesus Christ, we gain a
quality of life that is larger than death. Death
becomes not the end of life, but the door into a
larger life. People call our world "the land of the living." We might better call it "the land of the dying."
We begin to die the moment we are born, and our
lives are an inexorable move toward death. But
those who have believed in Jesus Christ know that
when death comes, we do not pass out of the land
of the living but into the land of the living. We are
not on our way to death. We are on our way to life.
That's what it means to be born again. That's what
it means to have eternal life. That's what it means
to believe in Jesus Christ.

How did Jesus end His statement to Martha? He

asked, "Do you believe this?" With that question He brought her to the question of personal faith. The faith that leads to eternal life can never be a faith we have inherited from our grandparents or that we acquire from being around the pastor. It is a personal commitment each one of us must make.

To Jesus' question Martha gave a remarkable answer (v. 27): "Yes, Lord, I believe that you are the Christ, the Son of God, who was to come into the world." Compare that to Peter's great confession (Matthew 16:16). Jesus had asked him, "Who do you say I am?" Peter had responded, "You are the Christ, the Son of the living God." Jesus responded that upon that confession, that truth, the church would be built.

Martha understood the same truth. Where had she learned it? Had she sat at Jesus' feet? Had she listened to Him teach the crowds? Clearly this woman, though her faith was imperfect, grasped the central truth on which it could grow: Jesus is the One sent by God.

It is the same for us today. It is on the truth Martha spoke that day in Bethany 2,000 years ago that you and I come to the One who is the resurrection and the life. We cannot begin to grow until we see Jesus for who He is and come to Him as we are.

The story moves on. Martha returned to the house and, taking Mary aside, told her that the Teacher had arrived and asked for her. Mary got up quickly and went to meet Jesus. She, in turn, spoke the same words Martha had used: "Lord, if you had been here, my brother would not have died." The same words Martha had used, but with one omission. Martha had gone on to say, "But I know that even now God will give you whatever you ask." Martha, for all her shortcomings, spoke of her faith. Mary, in contrast, was overwhelmed by her grief. She had sat at Jesus' feet and learned from Him. But now in His presence she was wrung out with her all-consuming sorrow.

When we read the other Mary-Martha story in Luke 10, it appeared that Mary was the "spiritual" one and Martha was the "unspiritual" one. Now as we look at these same two women, we discover that practical Martha had understood enough to give a magnificent confession of faith in Jesus Christ. Mary, on the other hand, was too engulfed in her loss to do more than say, "Jesus, if you had been here, my brother would not have died."

Note how Jesus adjusted to each one's need. With Martha, even in a time of deep mourning, He spoke deep theological truth. With Mary, He sympathized. He met her where she was so that He could take her to a different level of faith. Thus it is with each of us. God starts with us where we are. But He doesn't leave us there. He moves us to a deeper level of faith.

The stage was now set. Four days had passed since Lazarus died. The usual Middle Eastern tomb was a cave with shelves cut in the rock on three sides. At the opening of the tomb a groove was made in the ground and a great wheel-shaped stone was set in the groove so it could be rolled across the entrance to the cave. For the Jews it was important that the entrance be well sealed. They believed that the spirits of the departed hovered around the tombs for four days, seeking entrance again into the body of the departed one. But after four days they left, because by then the body would be so decayed that they could no longer recognize it.

The mourners had followed Mary and now gathered in front of the cave. The customary point of view was that the more unrestrained the mourning, the more honor they paid to the dead. These who had come to comfort Mary and Martha were not quietly weeping with heads bowed. Instead, they honored Lazarus with unrestrained wailing, with hysterical shrieking.

Jesus stood in the midst of the crowd of mourners. In both verses 33 and 38 John described Him by using a Greek word that is not accurately translated in many Bibles. Jesus was more than "deeply moved." He shuddered with indignation.

Indignation at what? Jesus stood there that day as the Lord of life, the one who had just told Martha that He was the resurrection and the life. There He was face to face with all the effects of the Fall: death, human misery, broken hearts. He had come into the world to deliver us from death and condemnation. He knew that as He confronted and conquered death that day, the final conquest could come in only one way. He too would have to pass through death. He would have to taste its bitterness. He would have to die.

He shuddered—shuddered at the awfulness of death. He shuddered at the consequences of sin. He shuddered at the pain of alienation. He shuddered with indignation that any of this had to happen. And then He acted. He spoke four times.

Speaking to the mourners, He simply said, "Take away the stone" (John 11:39). Jesus could have told the stone to roll away without human help, but He didn't. Those who stood there that day were given that task. God works with an economy of divine power. He requires us to do what we can do. He tests us by involving us in His miracles. "Take away the stone."

Had the Jews standing there heard correctly? Take away the stone? Surely Jesus couldn't be serious! Martha echoed their thoughts when she protested, "But, Lord, by this time there is a bad odor, for he has been there four days." Martha just missed the point of that conversation out on the roadside. Jesus had to remind her, "Did I not tell you that if you believed, you would see the glory of God?" (v. 40). Jesus worked to raise Martha's faith to a higher level so that she could look beyond the earthly, the practical, and the mundane to see spiritual reality. "Take away the stone."

The second time Jesus spoke, it was to God:

Father, I thank you that you have heard me.

I knew that you always hear me, but I said this for the benefit of the people standing here, that they may believe that you sent me.

Martha had said she believed that. But did the others? Did Mary? Did the disciples? Jesus laid His divine claim on the line to lead people to faith.

The third time Jesus spoke, He addressed Lazarus: "Lazarus, come out!" (v. 43). The dead man stumbled out, his hands and feet wrapped with strips of linen and a towel around his face. The crowd fell back, awestruck. Were their senses playing tricks on their minds? They had seen a corpse carried into that tomb four days earlier. It could not be true that Lazarus was alive again!

Jesus had not prayed, "Father, raise him from death!" Nor had He said, "In the name of the Father, come out." He had told Martha that He was the resurrection and the life. He acted on His own authority. He was the Lord of life, so Lazarus came out.

The fourth time Jesus spoke, it was again to the astonished audience: "Take off the grave clothes and let him go" (v. 44). The gasping bystanders needed to touch Lazarus and see for themselves that he was not a ghost.

Two things happened. First, many of the Jews who had come to visit Mary put their faith in Jesus (v. 45). That was the immediate result. Second, word of this incredible miracle soon reached the religious leaders in Jerusalem. They saw Jesus as a threat to their power. They met to seal His fate with a sentence of death.

A sentence of death? Yes, for Him. But a sentence of life for all of us who believe. He is the resurrection and the life. The one who believes in Him will live, even though that person dies. Whoever lives and believes in Him will never die. Do you believe this?

The old storytellers in many lands tell of a fabulous bird, sacred to the sun, called the phoenix. This huge bird, covered with an iridescent rainbow of gorgeous feathers, had no equal on earth. Not only was no other bird so beautiful, but none other sang so sweetly nor lived so long. The storytellers could not agree on the age of the phoenix. Some said the bird lived for 500 years. Others said its life was more than 12,000 years long.

When those years ended, the phoenix made itself a nest of twigs from spice trees, set its nest on fire, and, with the nest, was consumed. Nothing remained except a scattering of ashes on the earth. But then, the storytellers said, a breeze caught those ashes and somehow from them there arose another phoenix, a new firebird even more splendid than the one that had died. He would spread his wings, they said, and he would fly up to the sun.

The storytellers spun this myth in the fond hope that somehow it could be true. They spoke to something deep within each of us, the longing that out of the destructive tragedies of life, something better, more magnificent might come. What the storytellers could only imagine contains a truth of which Jesus Christ is the reality. Just as the more glorious phoenix can rise only from the ashes of its dead self and ruined nest, so great faith rises only from our dashed hopes and ruined dreams.

"If God wants you to trust Him," wrote Donald Grey Barnhouse, "He puts you in a place of difficulty. If He wants you to trust Him greatly, He puts you in a place of impossibility. For when a thing is impossible, then we who are so prone to move things by the force of our own being can say, 'Lord, it has to be You. I am utterly, absolutely nothing.' "

Lazarus lived only to die again. A second time the sisters went to the tomb with the corpse of their beloved brother. This time there was no resurrection. But Jesus had taken Martha's theology and had given it vitality: "He who believes in me will live, even though he dies; and whoever lives and believes in me will never die." If you believe in a God of resurrection, you can face the cemetery and know that even out of death can come life. It is, in the words attributed to St. Francis of Assisi, in dying that we live.

But not all funerals lead to life. When Mae lost her only son, she lost sight of God and His power and love. She could not see that the phoenix rises from the ashes of the reality that life invades death. She forgot—or never knew—that Jesus Christ passed through death to conquer it for all time and eternity.

As we experience the pain of loss, we can miss the phoenix. Yet Jesus speaks the same words to us that He spoke to Martha 2,000 years ago on the road into Bethany: "I am the resurrection and the life." can trust God's perfect timing. We can trust His love. We can come through our difficult experiences stronger in faith and hope as we learn that God is there for us in our loss, in our sorrow. What we let Christ do in our situation makes the difference.

This chapter is excerpted from A Woman God Can Lead *by Alice Mathews, published by Discovery House Publishers* © *1998.*

NOTES

NOTES

NOTES

NOTES

NOTES